THE
TRAINING
GAME

THE
TRAINING GAME

AN INSIDE LOOK
AT AMERICAN RACING'S
TOP TRAINERS

KAREN M. JOHNSON

DRF Press
New York

Published by
Daily Racing Form Press
100 Broadway, 7th Floor
New York, NY 10005

ISBN: 978-1-932910-69-8
Library of Congress Control Number: 2009923455

Jacket and Text designed by Chris Donofry
Cover photos by Barbara D. Livingston

Printed in the United States of America

Statistical data and related information provided by:

EQUIBASE
COMPANY
The Thoroughbred Industry's Official Source for Racing Information
WWW.EQUIBASE.COM
821 CORPORATE DRIVE LEXINGTON, KY 40503-2794

This book is dedicated to my parents,
Phil and Mary Kay Johnson. Your absolute
devotion and faith in me made me the
person I am today. I miss you both.

Table of Contents

Acknowledgments

This book would not have been possible without the cooperation of the trainers profiled in these pages, who were incredibly generous with their time. It was an honor to tell the stories of these accomplished horsemen, whose dedication to their trade is inspirational.

I am also extremely grateful to my mentor, Steven Crist, who hired me for my first reporting job at *The Racing Times*. Thank you, Steve, for your faith in me then and now. Thanks also to Robin Foster, a dear friend for many years, who applied her unparalleled editing skills to this book.

To my amazing friends Caton and Doug Bredar, Valerie and Christophe Clement, John Dooley, Karen Hallberg, Matt Hegarty, and Johanna Metzler: You each have my best interests at heart, and your friendship means more to me than you can imagine.

A special thank-you to my buddy from across the pond, David Gutfreund, whose advice, candidness, insight, and encouraging words during the writing of this book kept me on track. Thank you for always being in my corner.

Thanks to Graham Ross at the Fair Grounds for being my "messenger" and to reporter Bob Fortus of the *Times-Picayune* for his help and Cajun hospitality.

Thanks also to Chris Donofry of *Daily Racing Form*, who did such a great job with the design, and Chuck Kuehhas for providing me with statistics.

My sister, Kathy, encouraged me to write this book. Her belief in me and the unconditional love she provides is reason enough to get up every day. My brother-in-law, Don, along with my nieces Carolyn and Emma, complete the winning family superfecta.

Foreword

Since I began covering horse racing in 1985, I have had the opportunity to interview scores of trainers.

Many of those years were spent working on a daily deadline for *Daily Racing Form* and *The Racing Times*. The nature of producing copy for a daily is such that a reporter is essentially getting sound bites from trainers on a variety of topics including, but not limited to, how their horses are progressing as they are being prepared to run, and where that next race will come.

Unquestionably, there have been many well-written features about various trainers and their horses, but due to space limitations in a paper, these articles usually just scratch the surface of the story.

Writing a book about some of the most accomplished trainers in the business appealed to me because it gave me the opportunity to learn more about their methods, quiz them about their thoughts on an array of racing-industry topics, and get to know more about what makes them tick.

The eight men profiled in *The Training Game* are among the best ever to tighten the girth on a horse. Between them they have won 13 Triple Crown races, 17 Breeders' Cup races, and through 2008, their horses had amassed more than $861 million in earnings in North America. As a group, they have won 12 Eclipse Award training titles and 36 divisional championships with their runners. Four of these trainers are already in racing's Hall of Fame, and the Hall will surely be calling on some of the others.

Their approaches to training represent a wide range of methods. Some have hundreds of runners, spread out over multiple locations; others run midsize operations with a couple dozen horses. They took many different roads to the racetrack, and their personalities, as you would imagine, are just as diverse. During the course of our interviews, I found that each of these men revealed something about himself and his training style that I would never have known if I hadn't written this book.

I hope you enjoy reading *The Training Game* as much as I did writing it.

One

Steve Asmussen

Steve Asmussen is not a person who can be easily labeled or summed up in a few words. He is a study in contrasts: an imposing six-footer with a large frame that belies the fact that he was ever a jockey; a product of a small-time, nomadic racetrack upbringing who built a stable that now numbers hundreds of horses in divisions around the country; a trainer who, at the age of 39, smashed a 28-year-old record for number of wins in a season, yet had never won a Triple Crown or Breeders' Cup race until he got his hands on a raw bundle of talent named Curlin; and an intense competitor who spent half a year on the sidelines for a drug positive in one of his horses, yet refused to fight the suspension in court.

Asmussen, whose multidivisional operation carried 250 to 300 horses in 2008, has had phenomenal and unparalleled success as a trainer of winners. In 2004, his 18th year training, Asmussen saddled

1

555 winners to eclipse Jack Van Berg's North American record of 496, which was set in 1976. In 2008, Asmussen became the first North American trainer to saddle 600 winners in a single year, finishing the season with 622. He also led the country in wins in 2005 and 2007, and likely would have done so in 2006 had it not been for a six-month suspension for medication positives in two of his runners. (He still wound up third.)

In the sport of Thoroughbred racing, however, quality—not quantity—is often used as a factor in determining the strength of a trainer's operation. The staggering number of wins that Asmussen had produced with his massive stable certainly was worthy of recognition, but no Breeders' Cup wins or victories in Triple Crown races or Eclipse Award winners were part of the equation.

Asmussen was a finalist for the Eclipse Award as top trainer in 2004, 2005, and 2007, but it wasn't until January 26, 2009, that he finally took home that prize for his record-breaking season in 2008 and the work he did with Curlin that year. Six months earlier, Asmussen said winning the award was something he contemplated.

"Yes, it is something I think about, because my brother won one," he said, referring to Cash Asmussen's award as the top apprentice jockey of 1979. "It's funny how the Eclipse Award is the exact opposite reason why we are in the game. We are in a competitive sport where the winner is decided upon by actually doing it—winning. The Eclipse Award is like figure skating, where you are judged on how you do it. It's a great accomplishment and great coffee-shop talk and all that, but everyone tells you 'Great job' when you have a horse that is 20 lengths the best and wins by 10. Great job is when you win with a maiden 10K claimer in the last race at Sam Houston one night. That's a great job—the horse you get that can't run who wins."

When Curlin came along in 2007, Asmussen's career entered another stratosphere. Curlin provided Asmussen with his first win in a Triple Crown race in the 2007 Preakness and his first Breeders' Cup victory in that year's Classic, and became the first horse the trainer guided to championship titles (Horse of the Year and 3-year-old colt). Curlin was Horse of the Year again in 2008, as well as champion older male. The year 2008 also marked the first time that Asmussen's horses led the nation in earnings, amassing $27,940,247, which included the purse money from Curlin's win in the $6 million Dubai World Cup.

Given Asmussen's bloodlines—a father who was a jockey, a mother who was a trainer, and an older brother who was a riding sensation on two continents—it would have been a shocker if he had not chosen a path that brought him to the racetrack.

Asmussen, who was born on November 18, 1965, in Gettysburg, South Dakota, was a racetrack kid in every sense of the word. If there was a stall to muck, a horse to walk, a horse to gallop, tack to clean, or anything else that was required to keep the family's small stable operating smoothly, Steve and Cash, who is older by 3½ years, were smack in the middle of it all. Their mother, Marilyn, trained mostly Quarter Horses when her sons were young, and the boys' father, Keith, rode. In the small-world department, Keith rode Quarter Horses in the early 1960s in South Dakota for a little-known trainer, D. Wayne Lukas, who would revolutionize the sport of Thoroughbred racing in the 1980s and 1990s.

The Asmussen clan spent a great deal of time on the road, racing their horses at tracks in the Southwest. Regular destinations were Ruidoso Downs and Sunland Park in New Mexico, and the rough-and-tumble fair circuit in Laredo, Texas, where the Asmussens settled permanently in 1967.

"We were all horses," Steve Asmussen said. "It was a very different time on the racetrack for me then. I came from a very much ma-and-pa barn, which at that level, us kids provided a lot of the help. Everybody pitched in to do as good as you could. There are great memories because it was all family. As the youngest, lowest on the totem pole in that regard, I got told what to do a lot. I think of those early days a lot. How you win together and how you lose together. When you get something done you really feel a sense of accomplishment for the whole family."

Cash was the first Asmussen to attain national fame, winning an Eclipse Award at the age of 17. His name was appropriate, given his achievements, and was the result of a legal change from Brian in 1977. The confident teenager took New York racing by storm, scoring back-to-back riding titles in 1979 and 1980. In 1982, Cash left the United States to launch an enormously successful assault on European racing; among his notable accolades overseas was receiving France's Golden Whip award (the first foreigner to earn that distinction) on five occasions. One of his most celebrated wins came in the 1991 Prix de l'Arc de Triomphe aboard Suave Dancer, a horse whose purchase was recommended by Cash and his father and who was broken at the Asmussen family's El Primero Training Center in Laredo. Asmussen retired from riding in 2001 with more than 3,000 career wins.

Today, Cash and his wife, Cheryl, along with Keith and Marilyn, own and operate El Primero, one of the largest Thoroughbred training centers in the United States. Late in 2008, Cash said he was "promoted" from assistant to trainer by Cheryl, who had been conditioning some of the family's horses. Cash's name began appearing regularly on the overnights at Retama Park in Texas and Oaklawn Park in Arkansas. And now,

Park and was inducted into the track's Hall of Fame in 2007.

Before the opening of Lone Star Park, Asmussen's stable got a boost when he began training for the late John Franks, who won four Eclipse Awards as the country's top owner during the 1980s and 90s. Franks had a mammoth racing and breeding operation that included stakes, allowance, and claiming horses, and Asmussen was among the brigade of trainers the owner employed in the mid-90s. Franks shipped his lesser-quality horses to the smaller venues—the kinds of tracks frequented by Asmussen—where they could be competitive. With a sizeable amount of Franks-owned horses in his barn, Asmussen's operation began to expand in size, and he won training titles in 1995 at Remington Park in Oklahoma and at the newly opened Retama Park.

But it was a speedy colt owned by brothers Bob and Lee Ackerley, by the name of Valid Expectations, who gained Asmussen recognition outside the Southwest. Asmussen met the brothers through a friend, and Cash and Keith recommended the purchase of Valid Expectations to the Ackerleys. The son of Valid Appeal was bought in 1995 for $225,000 out of an Ocala Breeders' Sales auction and, in racing vernacular, became Steve's first "big horse."

"When 'Valid' was bought, everything we had in training was at Sam Houston Race Park for the winter," Asmussen said. "Houston wasn't running for anything. It was the bottom rung. Valid propelled us out of there. He was my first graded stakes winner, my first stakes winner in Kentucky, and my first stakes winner in Arkansas, Louisiana, and New York."

Valid Expectations earned nearly $600,000 during a three-year campaign that saw him run at 13 tracks. His biggest wins from a record of 12-3-6 in 27 starts were the Grade 3 Derby Trial at Churchill Downs in 1996 and the Grade 3 Sport Page

Handicap at Aqueduct in 1996. He also won ungraded stakes in Arkansas and Louisiana, and placed in stakes in California, Florida, Illinois, Massachusetts, Virginia, and Texas. Aboard for three of Valid Expectations' wins was Cash Asmussen, who returned from Europe just to ride the colt. Twelve years after winning the Sport Page aboard Valid Expectations, Cash said joining forces with Steve for his younger brother's first graded victory in New York was an "emotional" moment in his career. "It's a day Steve and I will never forget."

Steve said a nifty thing about Valid Expectations was that he handled whatever was thrown his way, often exceeding the expectations of his trainer.

"He had to ship and run and win and keep company," he said. "He was so much the best horse in the barn. But I don't think he had the tools to prepare him for what was fixin' to happen. He had to do it on his own because he didn't have the tools to face what was thrown at him. He taught us a lot. I didn't realize at that stage [of my career] how improbable it was to have a horse like him."

Asmussen came to Fair Grounds racetrack in New Orleans for the first time during the 1995-96 season, largely because of Valid Expectations. In 1995, Valid Expectations won the Old Hickory and Sugar Bowl Stakes at the Louisiana track, and for the first time in his career, Asmussen ended the year with more than $1 million in stable earnings.

During his first foray to Fair Grounds, he only brought 20 horses, but in subsequent years the numbers increased and Asmussen won his first of seven training titles there in 2000-01 when he tied with Tom Amoss.

During the mid-1990s, Asmussen's stable grew exponentially, thanks to an influx of horses from Louisiana native John Franks and Texas residents Bob and Lee Ackerley, James Cassels, Bill and Corrine Heiligbrodt, and Bob and Cathy Zollars. For Asmussen, who hungered to train a massive stable, the increasing number of horses that came into his care afforded him the opportunity to expand his operation outside the Southwest and into New York, Kentucky, and Illinois.

Snuck In, owned by the Ackerley brothers, was Asmussen's first Preakness starter in 2000; he finished fifth. The following year, Asmussen saddled his first Kentucky Derby starter, Louisiana Derby winner Fifty Stars, to a ninth-place finish for the partnership of Zollars and Cassels.

Dreams Galore, owned by Gary Tanaka, became Asmussen's first Grade 1 winner by taking the 1999 Mother Goose at Belmont Park. As with Suave Dancer and Valid Expectations, the Asmussen family connection played a role in the development of Dreams Galore. She was bought as a yearling by Asmussen's father, who originally raced the filly and won a couple of stakes with her before selling to Tanaka.

More graded winners in the big leagues followed for Asmussen. Among his most notable stakes winners were Lady Tak (2004 Ballerina and 2003 Test at Saratoga), Cuvee (2003 Futurity at Belmont and 2003 Saratoga Special), Private Vow (2005 Futurity), Summerly (2005 Kentucky Oaks), and Bwana Charlie (2004 Amsterdam at Saratoga).

The best was yet to come, however, and it could not have happened at a better time. Curlin, the horse who would propel Asmussen to his greatest triumphs, arrived in the barn in February 2007, shortly after the conclusion of the darkest period of the trainer's career. Asmussen had recently returned from a six-month suspension for the presence of mepivacaine, a local anesthetic, in a losing favorite who ran in an allowance race at Evangeline Downs in Louisiana in March 2006. It is illegal to administer mepivacaine on race day, and the postrace sample for No End in Sight was far above the acceptable limit for a lingering trace amount, indicating that it had been given anywhere from one to 10 hours before post time.

The positive wasn't the first for Asmussen, who has also had overages for the anti-inflammatory medication Butazolidin and the anti-bleeding medication Lasix, and positives for the tranquilizer acepromazine. But the mepivacaine suspension, which was served concurrently with an acepromazine positive at Sunland Park in New Mexico, was the lengthiest penalty the trainer had received.

Asmussen, who was not at Evangeline Downs on the day of the race, said that the administration of mepivacaine had to be an accident. He testified before the Louisiana Racing Commission in June 2006 that he had asked a veterinarian to give No End in Sight two other drugs that day, but not mepivacaine. Those medications were also illegal on race day, but Asmussen said he did not know they were prohibited in Louisiana. (Medication rules vary from state to state.)

The veterinarian denied giving the filly either mepivacaine or the other drugs. There were times during the day of the race when No End in Sight was unsupervised, and the chairman of the Louisiana Racing Commission, Bob F. Wright, was later quoted in *Daily Racing Form* as saying that it "would likely never be known" who gave the mepivacaine to the filly. Under racing's absolute-insurer rule, however, a trainer is responsible for the condition of his or her horses, no matter what the circumstances.

"When all of it was happening, you felt extremely wronged," Asmussen said in August 2008. "Accused of giving a horse 750 times the legal limit of mepivacaine with a filly that was even money or less and who was going to the test barn no matter what. What are the odds of someone doing something so stupid? It just felt wrong."

Nevertheless, he chose not to pursue the commission's ruling in court, becoming increasingly frustrated as the process unfolded. As he described it, " . . . they can't even pronounce your name, and they are taking personal calls, walking out of the room. You know, the fact of it, at the end of it, six months from now, you are still you. They can't take that away from you.

"This is the most I said to defend it right here. You've got to be kidding me. If anyone is that ignorant to believe I did that, let's just keep them headed down the wrong road; they will never find their way. It was beyond belief."

The only upside to Asmussen's forced absence was that he was able to spend quality time with his wife, Julie, and their three young sons—Keith James, Darren Scott, and Eric Mark—at their home in Arlington, Texas, and with his family in Laredo. While he was on suspension, Asmussen's horses were trained by one of his assistants, Scott Blasi, and ran in Blasi's name.

But Asmussen's life is the racetrack, and the six-month suspension left him feeling very isolated, he said.

"You know aquarium fish? If you have a fish with an eye infection, do you know how you save it? If you leave it in there, the other fish will eat it and kill it. To save the fish, you have to get him and put him in a separate aquarium and treat the water. When his eye heals up, you can put him back with the other fish. Well, if you are the fish, you don't know why you are being chased. You don't know why you are being isolated. You don't know why you are being made sick. And when you get back to the aquarium, you still don't [understand] why any of that happened. So a lot of times, I felt like a guppy with an eye infection.

"I mean, I don't think we are supposed to understand everything that happens to us. But how you respond to it, is who you are. The whole time—the stewards' hearing, the commission hearing, everything—you are just absolutely going crazy with

'What should I do?' 'How is this going to affect everybody?' The responsibility you have to everything.

"You are not yourself. The fact you are not able to feel the way you normally do. That commission hearing, I think that was why I chose not to appeal it at the time. When you're fighting, they are winning. They just got you so stirred up, you can't think straight. And then as we were driving back to the airport from the commission meeting, a sense of peace and calm came over me because I got to call Julie. I was going home to walk in my own house and stuff. So how bad is that? You could have fought it more at the time but I thought, 'How good do I have it?' We are all witness to this game, and lucky to be involved in it. I was lucky as a kid in Texas and New Mexico, and I am lucky now. But there are all different levels of the game. Winning still feels good."

Asmussen declined to speak on the record about the effect, if any, his six-month suspension had on his business, other than to say, "You can only control [the horses] in the barn. The rest doesn't help you. You see a lot of people who are distracted by that stuff and who are not doing any good because of it."

In January 2007, around the same time Asmussen returned from his suspension, one of his most promising 3-year-olds suffered an injury. Tiz Wonderful, owned by Jess Jackson of California's Kendall-Jackson vineyards, was considered among the early favorites for the Kentucky Derby following his undefeated 2-year-old season, but rapped a tendon and was forced to the sidelines.

A few weeks later, Asmussen ran his only starter at the 2007 Gulfstream Park meet, Gunfight, in the Swale Stakes on the Donn Handicap undercard. The same day at Gulfstream, Asmussen watched a robust colt by the name of Curlin make a dazzling career debut for trainer Helen Pitts in a seven-furlong maiden special weight race, which he won by 12¾ lengths while earning a Beyer Speed Figure of 101.

Also watching the race on a TV monitor in Ocala, Florida, a five-hour drive from Gulfstream, was bloodstock agent John Moynihan, an advisor to Jackson. Moynihan called Asmussen, then Jackson.

"It wasn't luck that we found the horse," Moynihan later told Bill Dwyre of the *Los Angeles Times*. "Even a novice who saw that race knew there was something special there. Our luck was that we were able to buy him."

Once again, a family connection played a part in an Asmussen success story, although this time the family was that of Scott Blasi. Helen Pitts was dating Scott's brother, Greg, which made it easier for Moynihan to act quickly.

"Normally, in this situation, the trainer doesn't want to lose the horse and won't be helpful in any regard about a sale," he said, but Pitts gave him a phone number for one of the colt's owners, setting the transaction in motion. (Pitts and Blasi were married in September 2008.)

Less than a week after Curlin's phenomenal debut, a deal was struck with his original owner, Midnight Cry Stable, and the colt came under Asmussen's care. Bill Gallion of Midnight Cry Stable and his partner, Shirley Cunningham Jr., kept 20 percent of the son of Smart Strike, whose new owners were Jackson's Stonestreet Stable, Satish Sanan's Padua Stable, and George Bolton. The sale price was around $3.5 million.

"The first time I watched Curlin run, I couldn't believe what he did without trying," Asmussen recalled. "He is kind of like the story of racing. Tiz Wonderful, who was just an incredible 2-year-old, who beat Any Given Saturday in the Kentucky Jockey Club [Stakes], had suffered a tendon injury right after the first of the year—the 10th of January. If it wasn't for that happening, you wouldn't have been able to pursue Curlin. All we would have been doing was looking at Curlin as someone who was hard to beat, and trying to beat him with Tiz Wonderful.

"The only horse I ran at Gulfstream the whole meet was in the race after Curlin. It is just amazing how it all fell together. You can't get over those events; the horse I ran in the Swale, Gunfight, ran a disappointing race [fifth]. So two big disappointments, one being Tiz Wonderful's tendon and then a disappointing race by Gunfight, put us in this position, which is amazing when you think about it. Besides being in the right place at the right time, it was misfortune as well. If Tiz Wonderful doesn't suffer the tendon injury or he does so a month later, you're not in the same state of mind or the situation where you're trying to get it done."

With Curlin ensconced in Asmussen's barn at Fair Grounds, what the trainer saw in Curlin's debut began to reveal itself in his training.

"He was very young, mentally as well as physically," Asmussen said. "His appetite was good. His attitude was fine. But there wasn't a lot of effort to everything he did, and I don't think that rounded him to form until the summer of 2007, actually.

"I remember the first time I worked him. He just went along. You didn't ask for more, but you didn't get more. And then the second time we worked him it was the same. From a timing standpoint we felt good. Then we worked him with two of our more accomplished horses at the time, Appealing Zophie and Zanjero. They were prepping for the Silverbulletday and the Risen Star at the Fair Grounds. We worked Curlin in behind them because he had just one race, and we knew we definitely wanted to be in the 3-year-old mix. We had him behind horses and he settled nicely. When [jockey] Donnie Meche pulled him out at the head of the stretch, I wanted him to pick it up, and wanted the other two horses to be kept in hand. We felt very comfortable with their experience and how much they knew. Appealing Zophie was fourth in the Breeders' Cup as a 2-year-old, and Zanjero was second in the Remsen. We just wanted to hold them together. When Donnie pulled him out, and asked him to pick it up, Curlin just kind of opened his eyes. For lack of a better word, he just opened up like a kite. Donnie slapped him down with the stick once, and he immediately went to the other horses. That was the day when you were like, 'Okay, he's way better than average.' He had just picked up good horses really well. From that point on, you felt like you were holding aces."

After easy wins in the Rebel and the Arkansas Derby at Oaklawn Park, under jockey Robby Albarado, who rode Curlin in all his starts for Asmussen, the next stop was the Kentucky Derby.

Curlin became Asmussen's fourth starter in the race—he previously saddled Fifty Stars, Storm Treasure, and Private Vow to off-the-board finishes—but the trainer had never been there with a colt who generated the kind of buzz that surrounded Curlin. Flashy, powerful, and undefeated, the strapping chestnut colt had everyone talking, but he was up against the previous year's 2-year-old champion, Street Sense, and was facing some historical roadblocks as well: No horse in 125 years had won the Derby without making a start at 2, and none since 1915 had won the race off only three starts.

Curlin showed his "talent" in the Rebel and the Arkansas Derby, and his "inexperience," Asmussen said, in the Kentucky Derby, where he was sent off as the 5-1 second choice. He was steadied slightly during the charge past the stands the first time and was 14th after three-quarters of a mile. According to the official chart of the race, the colt then "made a bold run five wide approaching the final furlong but couldn't threaten the top two." Favored Street Sense was the winner by 2¼ lengths over Hard Spun, with Curlin another 5¾ lengths back in third.

The first leg of the Triple Crown put Curlin right on target for the Preakness.

"He looked good. Nice and relaxed," Asmussen said when Curlin worked a half-mile at Churchill Downs nine days after the Derby. "I'm very impressed with how much horse he is, how strong he is."

In the Preakness, Curlin showed not only his strength, but also his tenacity. He and Street Sense moved almost as a team to overtake Hard Spun and C P West on the turn for home, but then the Derby winner began to pull away from Curlin, who was running on the wrong lead. Suddenly Curlin swerved in slightly, changed leads, and came on again under vigorous urging by Albarado to wear down Street Sense and win by a head.

With the Triple Crown a lost cause, Street Sense's trainer, Carl Nafzger, opted to skip the Belmont Stakes, so there would be no rubber match between the Derby and Preakness winners. The Belmont still provided plenty of drama, however, thanks to Curlin and the filly Rags to Riches, who staged an epic battle through the stretch of the 1½-mile classic. Rags to Riches, a half-sister to the previous year's Belmont winner, Jazil, prevailed by a head.

Curlin handled the pressure of the Triple Crown beautifully, Asmussen said.

"What separates him more than anything is how he responds to what just happened," Asmussen said in an August 2008 interview. "The stress of a hard day affects horses, and we just haven't seen that with Curlin. I have worked horses with him— accomplished horses. You watch them cool out after the works, and you can tell that you shouldn't work them again with Curlin. You just don't see that look from him.

"Perfect example of that is Zanjero, who is just a top-class horse, and nothing but class. He ran in the Derby when Curlin did, and Zanjero comes back and he is blowing; he's tired and drinking water. It's kind of the Derby after the Derby because of all the build-up for a horse to the race. And Curlin came from the test barn, and he was just playing. It was funny because everyone was asking, 'Are you going to run back in the Preakness or wait?' If you're not going to run Curlin back, then who are you waiting on?

"I doubted that anyone felt like Curlin did after the Derby. And it proved to be right because of how resourceful he is. Off the Derby, being his fourth race, and then two weeks later to run against Street Sense and Hard Spun in the Preakness . . . I was so proud of that group of horses, as a whole, for what they accomplished. I think the company Curlin kept really stamps who he is."

Following the Belmont, and a third-place finish in the Haskell at Monmouth Park, Curlin won the Jockey Club Gold Cup over a talented field that featured odds-on favorite Lawyer Ron, one of the country's top older horses. Curlin ended the year with a brilliant victory in the Breeders' Cup Classic over a sloppy and sealed track at Monmouth Park, against an accomplished group that included Street Sense, Hard Spun, Lawyer Ron, and Any Given Saturday.

Curlin's fans were absolutely delighted and probably shocked in January 2008 when it was announced at the Eclipse Awards in Beverly Hills that the colt would return for a 4-year-old campaign. It was a refreshing twist: Rather than being whisked off to the breeding shed, which is often the standard procedure with a horse who had already achieved so much, the reigning

Horse of the Year would remain in training for another season.

Curlin had already proved he was the best horse in North America, so early in February 2008, Jackson, who now owned 80 percent of Curlin, with the remaining 20 percent retained by Midnight Cry, said the target was the $6 million Dubai World Cup. (Satish Sanan and George Bolton had sold their interests in the colt to Jackson after the Breeders' Cup.)

It was announced that Curlin would fly to Dubai in mid-February to have a race over the track before the World Cup, since his connections believed that he excelled when making his second start over a new surface, as he did in winning the Jockey Club Gold Cup following his first race at Belmont Park in the Belmont Stakes, and also at Monmouth Park in the Breeders' Cup Classic, after running in the Haskell a couple months earlier.

The tremendous faith that Asmussen has in his staff was revealed when he tabbed Scott Blasi to oversee Curlin's training in Dubai, while he remained in the United States. Also accompanying Curlin to the Middle East was his favorite and most trusted companion, lead pony Pancho, and regular exercise rider Carlos Rosas.

Asmussen would later say that any mention of Curlin's accomplishments, "from day one to this point," had to include Blasi and Rosas. "Curlin's comfort level with them and their understanding of him just continuously led Curlin in the direction we wanted, physically and mentally. Horses aren't game pieces; you can't pick them up and place them anywhere.

"Mr. Jackson and his wife, Barbara, and John Moynihan came to New Orleans over the winter after they decided to keep him training. Once it was decided upon going to Dubai, we thought about what would be best for the horse. Scott was in the meetings as well. We felt that going there ahead of time wouldn't be as strenuous on him mentally and physically as just going there and coming back. Collectively, we thought it was best to go over there and acclimate and be ready for when it happens and to have more horse for when it was done."

Curlin won his prep for the Dubai World Cup in the Jaguar Trophy Handicap—toting 132 pounds—against an over-matched field. Four weeks later, on a balmy evening in the desert, he annihilated 11 rivals to win the World Cup by 7¾ lengths. The Curlin team accomplished what they had set out to do: Prove their horse was a world champion.

There were a few minor hiccups for the Curlin camp during the summer of 2008, including a licensing issue involving the Midnight Cry Stable crew—attorneys Gallion and Cunningham—who were in jail while on trial for defrauding clients of $64 million won from a diet-drug lawsuit. Ultimately, the licensing matter was ironed out and did not interfere with Curlin's race schedule.

After winning the Stephen Foster in mid-June, his first race since the World Cup, Curlin was tried on the turf in the Man o' War at Belmont Park as a prelude to an even loftier goal: It was hoped that he would show enough ability on that surface to punch his ticket to France for Europe's premier grass race, the Prix de l'Arc de Triomphe in October. Although he didn't run poorly in the Man o' War—he finished second to the 2006 Breeders' Cup Turf winner, Red Rocks—Curlin was clearly not as dominant on the turf as he was on the dirt. So it was back to the main track for Saratoga's Woodward, which Curlin won en route to notching his second victory in the Jockey Club Gold Cup. With that triumph, he became the first North American-based runner to reach and surpass $10 million in career earnings.

There was only one big year-end prize remaining: the $5 million Breeders' Cup Classic, which Curlin had won in 2007 to lock up his Horse of the Year award. Throughout 2008, however, his connections had not committed to running in that event because it was being held for the first time on a synthetic surface, something Curlin had never tried. Less than an hour after the Gold Cup, Jackson ended the suspense by telling reporters that the colt would be sent to California the next morning to train over Santa Anita Park's newly installed Pro-Ride surface, with one caveat: If Curlin didn't appear at ease over the synthetic track in the mornings, he would not defend his title in the Classic.

The Curlin camp's hesitation was understandable. Synthetic surfaces were a recent development on the American racing scene, and the early reviews were mixed. Though synthetics were supposed to provide safer racing conditions and a more consistent surface, impervious to track biases and the vagaries of weather, they were not the cure-all that their promoters had hoped for, and many owners and trainers were leery of risking a top-class horse's reputation on an unknown entity. Synthetic tracks were not, as originally billed, immune to extremes of weather, and Santa Anita's first artificial surface, Cushion Track, proved to be such a disaster that it was ripped out in the summer of 2008 and replaced with an entirely new alternative, Pro-Ride.

Even though Asmussen has divisions at several tracks where synthetics are used—Keeneland, Presque Isle Downs, and Woodbine—he said artificial surfaces can be confounding.

"I don't think you ever know where you are at with one," he said. "From a handicapping point of view, no one knows where they are at. It changes from race to race, day to day, let alone track to track."

If Curlin ran in the Classic, it was expected that he would face

2008 Kentucky Derby and Preakness winner Big Brown in a much-anticipated matchup that would bring the colts together for the first time. Big Brown didn't make the Classic because of a hoof injury, but Curlin did. Sent off as the 4-5 favorite, he made a sweeping move on the turn to take a short lead, but faded in the stretch and finished fourth. The winner was Raven's Pass, a European invader who had raced exclusively on turf.

Asmussen ascribed the defeat to the synthetic surface, saying, "It was a turf race. It absolutely was the Pro-Ride surface." Whether it was that or the toll of a long, arduous campaign, Curlin failed to display the same effectiveness that he did on conventional tracks, just as in the Man o' War. The Classic was his final race, and he entered stud at Lane's End Farm in Kentucky in 2009.

Before Curlin left for Lane's End in November, Churchill Downs gave the colt and his connections a proper send-off. Asmussen was so focused on what it would feel like when Curlin left his barn for his second career in the breeding shed that he wasn't prepared for the emotions that caught him "off guard" when the colt was paraded before an enthusiastic crowd at Churchill.

"Curlin was a very special horse, and I don't think it was anything we did for him, it was what he did for us," Asmussen said. "When he got beat in the Breeders' Cup, we worried about how he felt. I hope to have a horse that someone has to try to compare to Curlin. That would be a huge compliment if someone had to say that. You know, there are several horses you can't replace for several reasons—Valid Expectations and Lady Tak are another two that come to mind. They were horses that did things for you that you couldn't do for yourself."

The spectacular 22-month run by Curlin was the focal point

of the stable, at least from a media standpoint. But Asmussen also had hundreds of other runners to manage when Curlin was making headlines.

In August 2008, Asmussen, who maintains a year-round presence in New York, had horses at Saratoga, Belmont Park, Lone Star Park, Arlington Park, Evangeline Downs, Monmouth Park, Woodbine, and Presque Isle Downs. At other times of the year, there are divisions in place at Churchill Downs, Keeneland, Fair Grounds, Retama Park, Sunland Park, Oaklawn Park, Remington Park, Delta Downs, and Sam Houston Race Park.

Asmussen probably spends as much time in the air as he does on the ground. He boards planes weekly to check on his various divisions.

"In 2004, I tried to stay on a schedule and it was very taxing, especially mentally," he said. "So then I made the decision to go wherever I think I need to be, as opposed to a set plan where you weren't comfortable. My wife makes all my travel plans."

It's not unusual for Asmussen to have double-digit starters at tracks across the country on a single day. He might be running in a $1 million stakes in New York while another of his horses is competing for an $11,000 purse in a maiden claimer at a track in the Southwest.

Claimers are an integral part of Asmussen's operation. Of his 4,541 career wins through 2008, 1,402 were in claiming races. He said his awareness of his competition at a multitude of tracks is helpful in making claims.

"A lot of it is that you run with those horses you might be looking to claim, so you kind of have a value on them in your head that day," Asmussen explained. "I think having a lot of horses gives you an idea of who you are running against. How we claim some of the horses we have is the same reason people bet on horses. We're betting they are worth the money and they are betting to win. It is a huge advantage having so many [starts] with our horses, that even with the bad claims you find a softer spot in an easier place so you retrieve some of your investment. I love [to claim] horses."

Asmussen sometimes claims a runner for himself, and one of his favorites is Red Rock Creek, who was among 10 horses the trainer saddled on an 11-race card at Fair Grounds one afternoon in January 2009. Red Rock Creek finished sixth in a $100,000 stakes that afternoon, but Asmussen had already made good on his initial investment with the gelding. Claimed for $10,000 as 6-year-old in June 2006 at Lone Star Park, Red Rock Creek had won 17 races, including a stakes at Retama Park, and was graded-stakes-placed before running that day at Fair Grounds.

Asmussen recalled that in 2004, the year he broke the training record for number of wins, he was also the fourth-leading owner in the country in that category, and claimed seven horses for himself at Fair Grounds in one day alone. In contrast, he had just 37 wins as an owner in 2008.

"Obviously, things have changed," he said. "Not that I wouldn't claim; I have nothing against it. It's just not something I've been actively doing for myself lately."

In 2008, Asmussen estimated he had about 30 owners, many of whom are involved in partnerships. Among his clients are Heiligbrodt Racing Stable, Vinery Stables, Winchell Thoroughbreds LLC, Zayat Stables, Bob and Cathy Zollars, and Oceanfront Property Stable, a partnership that includes country-music star George Strait.

"I have the greatest core of owners with a great connection; with a very high comfort level of who we are and what we are trying to do. I think everyone involved with us knows how important their horses are to us.

"The owners complement each other. They race at different levels," he continued, adding that coming from a racing family that was involved with a high volume of horses taught him how to manage such a diverse stable. "You just evaluate the horses and get them to a certain level, and place them at the level where they can earn the most money. Whatever day is their best race, they are never going to be worth more money," he said.

"I'm very proud of the long-term relationships we have from an owner-trainer standpoint, especially in this day and age. If you do the best thing for the horse, it's the best thing for the owner all the time."

Some of Asmussen's clients are breeders, while others acquire their horses at sales. He said he has a fairly basic formula for selecting horses at auction.

"Pick the one that looks like Michael Jordan," he said. "That's the goal, the idea, and what we are trying to do. Going to the sales is like handicapping; just at a higher level. You try to be bright. You test yourself. It drives my wife crazy; I have sales catalogues everywhere in the house."

Many horses trained by Asmussen receive their pre-racing education at El Primero. That is certainly an advantage for the trainer, who has a constant and open dialogue with his family, and therefore has a handle on what to expect from a young horse when it comes into his barn. His brother, Cash, described the transition of moving horses from El Primero to Steve's barn as "a smooth handoff."

Keith Asmussen said what the babies reveal to him at El Primero will determine their position in Steve's stable.

"When we breeze them, the cream comes to the top, and for those horses, Steve can choose bigger tracks. The lesser ones go down the line to [smaller] tracks. Some don't ever get to the races, and I call up an owner and tell them to take the horse home."

With the breadth of Asmussen's operation, having the right staff is essential in keeping the stable running efficiently. To that end, he has surrounded himself with assistants whom he not only trusts, but also considers part of his family—people like Scott Blasi, Toby Sheets, and Darren Fleming.

"When you think about Scott being with us for [12] years and what we have accomplished together, it is just tremendous," Asmussen said. He pointed out that his middle son's name is Darren Scott, "so that tells you something."

He added, "Darren Fleming I have known since the mid-80s, I worked with him in Oklahoma, galloping. Toby Sheets, a long-time assistant, is a childhood friend of Darren's, and Darren brought him around.

"I'm looking for [staff] who care. It's all about the horse. The horse is the reason we are here. It isn't just about me; there are so many people involved with what you get done. For anybody to run a dozen horses, there are 50 people involved. To run any horse and to think of all the people involved, it's pretty amazing.

"I'm very uncomfortable taking credit I don't deserve. It's be humble or get humble in this game. It's just the sense of pride on people's faces when a horse wins, and how many people that just made happy. Their constant efforts and all that is expected of them . . . None of this would happen without them."

Asmussen laughed when he was asked how many employees he has and what his weekly payroll is. "There's a lot and it's a lot."

Blasi, who is eight years younger than Asmussen, said the job, which regularly requires 14-hour days, is not for everybody.

"It's high-pressure," he said. "There are so many things we try to manage to make things as smooth as we want it. I first started galloping for Steve at Remington. To see where [the stable] has gone since and everything we've went through to get to this place . . . there is a lot of emotion involved. The fighting and everything you do to get to this point. The hard part is staying on top. Not every day is a great day. Mistakes are made. You try to be as perfect as possible.

"The one thing about working for Steve is that from the outside it seems like so much. A lot of people come up to me and say, 'I don't know how you do it.' When you're in the middle of it, it doesn't seem overwhelming. I personally like the work because I don't do well [with idle time], so it's a good job for me. When you're an assistant in this type of organization, you have to pay attention to what is in front of you and be able to train horses. Steve is very organized, and we go over every horse, every day. But he doesn't hold your hand. We both learned some of the same things at the same time—what you want to do and what you don't want to do. We are a lot better at it than we were 12 years ago."

Blasi said beyond the working relationship he has with Asmussen, there is friendship.

"I think everybody has a certain amount of people they choose to confide in," Blasi said. "Steve and I definitely have that kind of relationship. Whether it's business or personal, Steve has been a very good friend to me."

Asmussen admits that at times he is difficult to deal with. Rages have landed him in trouble with racing officials, who have fined him for confrontations he has had on the track, and it's not unusual for Asmussen to angrily and publicly confront jockeys when he finds fault with their rides.

By his own admission, he is a bad loser.

"I'm horrible. I'm horrible," he said. "I'm way more surprised by the races we lose than the ones we win. Winning is what you were expecting and what you planned on doing. So losing . . . I'm just horrible with that."

Nevertheless, he once again cited his racetrack upbringing

as an advantage in dealing with the day-to-day stress of a singularly demanding profession.

"In that sense, I think I'm fortunate to have grown up in a racing family—seeing the disappointments [my parents] had on a race-to-race basis, the work ethic that they had to get up every morning and do a good job to put together as many winners as they could. That philosophy has enabled our stable to be in this position. You don't like losing and you take it bad, but the alarm goes off and you get up and go.

"No matter how good you do, you don't get a head start. No matter how bad you do, they don't put you behind the gate. That is what I love about racing. It is not judged. The first one to the wire wins. You just have to put yourself in position.

"But [losses] are going to happen, so you do your best and try to get good races out of them and you become proud of horses' efforts. But you are going to get beat, so you just wake up and try to hope for the best.

"I've made horrible mistakes—embarrassing personality mistakes," he continued. "I imagine my wife and kids have felt the brunt of it unjustly. It's something like everything else in life that you work on and try to adjust. I've acted a fool with a lot of people [when I lost]. I probably acted a fool with a lot of people when I'm winning. I've taken the approach there are two people in everybody. Who they really are and who they are pretending to be, and I want mine to be as close together as they possibly can.

"I remember in 1994, I wasn't pleased with where I was in my life and what I was doing. I felt capable of better. I guess it was a chance encounter, if you want to call it that. A Catholic priest told me, 'Wake up in the morning and do as well as you can. Put enough of those days together, and you will be surprised as to where you end up.' A day doesn't go by that I don't think about that. I just try to address what there is today, good or bad, and start again tomorrow. Life isn't overwhelming, unless you allow it to overwhelm you."

Cash said one of Steve's strengths is his drive to always do the best he can with his stable and for his owners. He said his brother's approach to that end is not always subtle.

"You send Steve Asmussen on a mission, the mission will be accomplished," Cash said. "And there will be a lot of trees torn down on the way."

Personality aside, there is the perception by some in the industry that Asmussen doesn't play by the rules. Detractors point to his medication infractions. In June 2008, the Texas Racing Commission cited Asmussen for the presence of hydroxy-lidocaine, a metabolite of lidocaine, in a horse who had won at Lone Star Park two months earlier. Texas has a zero-tolerance policy for prohibited medications, with the exception of permissible levels of Butazolidin and Lasix. The matter continued to be litigated in 2009 by Asmussen's attorneys, one of whom is the high-profile Thoroughbred owner Maggi Moss, who led the country in wins in 2007 and has horses with the trainer.

When Asmussen was asked how he would respond to those who question his integrity as a trainer, he said his winning percentage is in line with what you would expect from such a large operation, which features horses well spotted at multiple locales on a daily basis.

"I hover around 20 to 21 percent, which you know, you win that many races and you lose that many races. You just can't give up, you keep going over there and you are constantly trying to assess the ability of your horses. You want them mentally and physically ready for what you want them to do. And you want to put them in with horses they can beat. That's our goal and we are trying to do that constantly. That's why we are at so many

STEVE ASMUSSEN

VITAL STATISTICS

CATEGORY	STS.	W%	ROI
1stNAStart	5	0	0
1stAfterClm	62	0.27	2.02
2ndAfterClm	43	0.26	1.57
1stRaceTrn	172	0.22	1.5
180+Trn	87	0.21	1.57
61-180Trn	263	0.21	1.68
2nd45-180Lay	402	0.21	1.39
2nd180+Lay	79	0.22	1.42
1-7Last	26	0.35	1.68
1stStart	314	0.17	1.54
2ndMdn	246	0.26	2.05
MSWtoMCL	81	0.3	2.23
1stTurf	124	0.11	1.17
1stBlink	34	0.21	1.38
1stLasix	42	0.17	1.5
2YO	757	0.21	1.66
Dirt/Turf	171	0.11	1.09
Turf/Dirt	210	0.25	1.6
BlinkOn	38	0.21	1.42
BlinkOff	21	0.14	0.87
Sprint/Route	263	0.24	1.86
Route/Sprint	209	0.22	1.65
Sprint2/Route	51	0.24	1.75
31-60Days	1071	0.21	1.47
WonLast	611	0.18	1.34
Wet	339	0.26	1.78
Dirt	2323	0.23	1.59
Turf	418	0.14	1.23
Sprints	2164	0.21	1.45
Routes	1097	0.2	1.46
MCL	307	0.27	1.91
MSW	735	0.23	1.64
Claim	775	0.22	1.44
ALW	791	0.17	1.29
STK	559	0.16	1.23
GSTK	139	0.14	1.15
DebutMCL	49	0.22	1.72
Debut>=1Mile	19	0.05	0.56
Synth	520	0.13	1.06
Turf/Synth	47	0.15	1.1
Synth/Turf	49	0.14	1.79

*January 1, 2008, through February 8, 2009, North American runners only

CAREER HIGHLIGHTS

BREEDERS' CUP

STARTS	1ST	2ND	3RD
13	1	1	2

WINNERS
Curlin: Classic (2007)

TRIPLE CROWN

STARTS	1ST	2ND	3RD
13	1	1	1

WINNERS
Curlin: Preakness (2007)

ECLIPSE AWARDS
Leading Trainer (2008)
Curlin: Horse of the Year (2007, 2008);
   3-Year-Old Colt (2007); Older Male (2008)

RECORDS/NOTABLE ACHIEVEMENTS
Set North American record for most wins in 2004 (555).

Set North American record for most wins in 2008 (622).

Leading trainer by wins in 2002 (407), 2005 (475), and 2007 (488).

Set record for races won in one day in 2004 (10 from a combined 17 starters at Delta Downs, Fair Grounds, Oaklawn Park, Sam Houston Race Park, and Sunland Park).

Reached 4,000 career wins on February 17, 2007, with J J's Bud at Oaklawn Park.

CAREER SUMMARY

STS.	1ST	2ND	3RD	EARNINGS
21,941	4,601	3,706	3,130	$134,173,720

*Through February 8, 2009, North American runners only

tracks: You are trying to find the spot that makes them the winner. I think anyone who is a horseman can walk in our barn and see why we win. Why does Curlin win? Look at him. I'm very proud of the caretakers we have here, and how blessed I am with talented and qualified help.

"I remember going to France to visit Cash. He was all of it there. He was doing Coca-Cola commercials. He was such a big deal over there. After the races, walking in the grandstand, you could hear people saying, 'Cash, you're the greatest,' and all that. Being his brother, I was impressed. Then Cash told me the same guy last week told him he was the worst he had ever seen. I didn't believe Cash at the time, but that stuck with me.

"You know when people tell you [that] you are great at something? They are not qualified. The same people who were knocking you before you were this good, they weren't qualified then, either. It just matters what you think. You know when it was a good job and when it wasn't. That moment with Cash was the moment that I knew [outsiders] weren't the judge. It's about how proud it makes the people who matter. What else would you want?

"The best feeling I have when I lay down to sleep is how proud my parents, wife, and kids are of me. Racing is very special in that way because my family is such a big part of it. The sense of pride that everyone feels and outwardly shows, whether they are trying to or not to show it, is what is special and matters to me. You realize how blessed you are to have your families in your life. At the end of the day, it's the only thing that matters."

Two

Rick Dutrow

If you're looking for the human equivalent of an inkblot test, Rick Dutrow Jr. just might be it. Everyone sees something different in the controversial trainer, and the adjectives that have been used to describe him range from *arrogant, brash, cocky,* and *loudmouthed* to *accessible, brilliant, candid,* and *laid-back.* Love him or hate him, everyone has an opinion about Dutrow.

At his lowest point, he was living in a tack room on the Aqueduct backstretch, yet little more than a decade later, no one in the sport of Thoroughbred racing was flying higher. Dutrow had trained Big Brown to brilliant victories in the Kentucky Derby and the Preakness Stakes, but with racing's first Triple Crown victory in 30 years seemingly within reach, the colt turned in an inexplicably terrible performance in the Belmont Stakes. In a way, Dutrow's roller-coaster ride in 2008 was a distillation of the extraordinary highs and lows he has experienced throughout his life.

Before Big Brown's wins in the Kentucky Derby and Preakness, Dutrow had already established himself as a top-class horseman. He trained Saint Liam, the 2005 Breeders' Cup Classic winner, who was voted 2005 Horse of the Year and champion older male; 2005 Breeders' Cup Sprint winner Silver Train; 2007 Breeders' Cup Mile winner Kip Deville; 2008 Dubai Golden Shaheen winner Benny the Bull; and 2008 Godolphin Mile winner Diamond Stripes. In New York, his home base of operation, Dutrow won three year-end training titles and finished second on four other occasions. Through 2008, he had saddled more than 1,300 winners and his runners had amassed $65 million in purse money.

The drive and dedication that spurred Dutrow to those accomplishments was not always there. He was once leading a life that was on the fast track to nowhere.

Born on August 5, 1959, Dutrow is the son of the late Dick Dutrow, a respected and successful trainer on the Mid-Atlantic circuit who primarily operated a claiming stable. The elder Dutrow eventually moved to New York, where he continued to do well with claimers in the 1980s. One of his best horses was King's Swan, who was claimed for $80,000 and wound up earning nearly $2 million by the time he retired at age 10 as "the King of Aqueduct," though he also had wins in Belmont Park's prestigious Vosburgh and the Tom Fool Handicap to his credit.

Growing up, Rick and his brothers, Tony and Chip, spent a great deal of time in the barn of their father, who led the nation in 1975 with 352 wins, then a North American record. Nearly a decade after Dick Dutrow's death, he still ranked 13th on the list of all-time leading trainers by races won.

Each of Dick Dutrow's sons became a trainer. Tony, who won his 1,000th career race in October 2007, is a prolific presence on the Mid-Atlantic circuit. Chip, who trained briefly in 2002 and 2003, returned to training in the fall of 2008 after assisting Tony and Rick for several years.

Despite receiving a hands-on education in his father's shed row, Rick didn't immediately choose to put it to good use. He wanted to party, and as a result, his record in his early days of training was dismal. He saddled his first horse in 1979; his first winner would not come until 1986. From 1979 through 1997, Dutrow had a meager eight winners from 72 starters. In several of those years, he didn't even start any horses.

During Dutrow's wild days, which were fodder for the press during Big Brown's Triple Crown quest, he used drugs, was flat-out broke, and lived in a tack room at Aqueduct. In 1997, he was shocked into the realization that something had to change when Sheryl Denise Toyloy, the mother of his daughter, Molly, was murdered while the 2-year-old was in another room of the house Toyloy shared with her boyfriend, Richard Vale. Dutrow was not involved with Toyloy at the time of her death, which took place during a robbery carried out by drug dealers, but he was still devastated. Molly later came to live with Dutrow in his Aqueduct tack room, but Rick's mother, Vicki, wisely stepped in, and the child went to live with her in Maryland. Molly, who was 13 years old during Big Brown's Triple Crown run, now lives with her father in his East Norwich home on Long Island.

As a result of Dutrow's lifestyle choices, his relationship with his father was severely strained. The elder Dutrow disapproved of everything that had brought his middle son to that low point in his life. Dick was particularly upset about Rick's relationship with Toyloy, who also used drugs.

Dick Dutrow died in February 1999 from pancreatic cancer. His death came the same year that Rick got the ball rolling on his career.

"I can't say that yes, I made amends with Dad," Dutrow said.

"His mind wasn't right toward the very end; the [cancer] was eating him alive. I want to hope that we did, but I can't be sure. I don't look back and think we ended in the wrong way or wake up in the middle of the night thinking about it. I've always been the easiest type of guy to get along with, and I want to be under the impression I got along with Dad at the end."

Rick Dutrow and his two brothers are separated by one year in age—Tony is the eldest and Chip is the youngest—and as they grew up they worked alongside their father. Rick, a high-school dropout, credits Dick Dutrow for giving him a very valuable education of another sort.

"First we learned all the basic stuff from Dad, like how to walk a horse and how to groom a horse," he explained. "Later, when you had a little problem with a horse's leg, I learned whether you should ice it or hose it or put it in a tub and soak it. My dad had so many horses, which meant many situations would come up.

"Dad was an excellent horseman. Me and my brothers would just sort of learn as we went along," he continued. "There was plenty of opportunity to see all the good and bad things racing had to offer. Dad always had 100 horses. We got well-schooled with the opportunity to see a lot of things. It's not like Dad had five horses. When you have so many horses, you are going to hit a lot of problems and you are going to see all those problems and figure out what to do with them and to make it best for the horses. By the time I was 15, 16, I was the foreman."

Dutrow recalled that his father's course in Horsemanship 101 did not include many lectures or Q-and-A sessions.

"When you were with Dad in the barn, you didn't have to ask questions. All you had to do was watch and see. When I went on my own, and something came up, I would call Dad. But while I was in his barn, I didn't ask Dad a lot of questions, I just watched and learned," he said. "Dad had good assistants, good

The partnership between Dutrow and Goldfarb turned out to be a productive one. Goldfarb was the leading owner in New York by number of races won in 2001, 2002, and 2003, and Dutrow led the trainers' standings in that category in 2001 and 2002, and again in 2005. He was on his way, with a growing client base and higher-class horses, but as his successes mounted, so did questions about how he was achieving them— a sentiment that would be summed up by racing columnist Andrew Beyer during Big Brown's run through the American classics in the spring of 2008.

"After Dutrow acquires new horses, he seemingly has the power to transform them magically. . . . When a trainer does this once, it's a remarkable feat. But when he improves horses dramatically on a regular basis, he will be suspected of taking some unfair edge. Dutrow does it on a regular basis. Over the past five years, the horses he has claimed have won an astonishing 35 percent of the time in the first start for his barn."

Is Dutrow's winning touch the result of medicine, magic, or mental telepathy? In 2008, Goldfarb told John Scheinman in the *Washington Post*, "We would walk down the shed row, and he'd stop and look at a filly and say to the groom, 'Take that filly's temperature.'" Sure enough, Goldfarb said, the horse would be running a fever.

Bloggers flooded the Internet in 2008 with their take on Dutrow. The same brashness that won over Sandy Goldfarb had a polarizing effect on people: They either found Dutrow refreshing or were completely turned off by him. Many said they couldn't root for Big Brown because his trainer was a loudmouth with a checkered past who illegally medicated his horses. Those in the trainer's corner said he did brilliant work with Big Brown—who had to be nursed through chronic quarter cracks—to have him ready to win the Derby easily after only three lifetime starts. When Dutrow opined it was a "foregone conclusion" that Big Brown would win the Belmont Stakes, his supporters said he was just showing faith in his horse; his critics, who outnumbered his fans, believed he was unnecessarily belittling the competition.

The trainer ignited yet more controversy with his comments that his veterinarians injected each of his horses every month with the anabolic steroid Winstrol, which was then legal in most racing jurisdictions, including the states where the Triple Crown races were run. Dutrow added that he didn't know what Winstrol was used for—a curious statement coming from a horseman who had been around for as long as he had.

The use of steroids in other sports—chiefly Major League Baseball—had already been under intense scrutiny for several years, and now it was horse racing's turn. In addition, the death of Derby runner-up Eight Belles, who had fractured both front ankles while galloping out after the race and had to be euthanized at Churchill Downs, had focused unprecedented attention on the health and welfare of Thoroughbreds.

Reporters had a field day with Dutrow's comments regarding Winstrol, which many people perceived as being linked to his own history of various medication positives—not only those pertaining to horses he had trained, but also his own drug violations (eight for marijuana). The list of offenses on file with the Association of Racing Commissioners International was indeed lengthy, but many were administrative violations or duplications. Among his most significant infractions, however—outside his personal drug use—were equine positives for mepivacaine and clenbuterol, for which he received suspensions and fines. Dutrow's other transgressions included overages for Butazolidin, Lasix, and clenbuterol; false workout information concerning future Queen's Plate winner Wild Desert, who was credited with being at Monmouth when in fact he was at Aqueduct; and communicating with his stable when he was suspended, which is not allowed.

Dutrow often seems to be in hot water, partly due to his self-acknowledged manner of speaking "from the gut." That inability to think before he talks landed him in plenty of hot water in 2008. *How Not to Make Friends* could have been the title of a book filled with the comments Dutrow made to the press during and after the Triple Crown campaign. Among his bigger gaffes was his criticism of John Servis's training of Smarty Jones in preparation for the 2004 Belmont Stakes. On a National Thoroughbred Racing Association teleconference before the 2008 Belmont, Dutrow was asked if he was worried that other jockeys in the race would "gang up" on Big Brown and rider Kent Desormeaux. Pat Forde of ESPN.com posed the question, "There are some people who believe that that is exactly what did happen to Smarty Jones in 2004. Do you have any recollection of that race and think that that might have occurred?"

In part, Dutrow responded, "I think maybe the way that [Servis] trained that horse for that race, going up to the Belmont, had a lot to do with him getting beat. I was at my house and they showed a flash to where Smarty Jones was breezing for the Belmont—he did it at Philadelphia Park, on a sloppy, sealed track. That just blew my mind away. I just could not imagine that anybody would do that with a horse, especially one going for the Triple Crown."

For the record, Smarty Jones did not breeze on a sloppy, sealed track in preparation for the Belmont.

"I don't have anything against John Servis; I didn't knock John," Dutrow said four months after making those comments. "I thought he did a great job with Smarty Jones. I just answered a question, and I always answer from the gut."

Asked if he regretted anything he said on the record in 2008, Dutrow, who was called to Capitol Hill to provide testimony at a summer congressional hearing regarding steroids but canceled because he said he was sick, responded, "I don't see that I said anything wrong. They asked me if gave steroids and I told them Big Brown got Winstrol. I didn't bring up the issue, they did, and it's not a big deal because you [were] allowed to use Winstrol.

"You know, I first got myself in trouble by telling everyone I was going to win the Derby. What the hell. I was asked, 'Do you like your horse?' 'Yeah, I like my horse.' 'Do you think you are going to win?' 'Yeah, I think I am going to win; of course I do.' It was as simple as that. I liked him in the Derby; I thought it was a mismatch. We knew by far we had the best horse. They asked me questions and I answered it. That's all it was, babe."

Dutrow, who calls everyone babe, men and women alike, smiled when he thought back to the days leading up to the Kentucky Derby. Big Brown was targeted for the Derby as soon as he came into Dutrow's barn in the fall of 2007. The colt was originally trained by Pat Reynolds, but after the bay son of Boundary annihilated a field of maidens on the turf at Saratoga on September 3, 2007, owner Paul Pompa Jr. sold a 75 percent interest in Big Brown to International Equine Acquisitions Holdings Stable. The terms of the sale, with a purchase price believed to be around $3 million, called for Big Brown to be transferred to Dutrow, who already trained for IEAH.

Big Brown's new connections had hoped to run him in the inaugural Breeders' Cup Juvenile Turf at Monmouth Park, but quarter-crack problems prevented him from racing again until March 5, 2008, at Gulfstream Park. He won a first-level allowance race, originally carded for the turf, by a breathtaking 12¾ lengths.

"When he won the first race for us . . . that was an overpow-ering race," Dutrow said. "I think he became the Kentucky Derby favorite in that race. Everybody in the racing world saw that that was an unbelievable race. He had only three easy breezes going up to that. It was crazy."

The day entries were taken for the grass race, Dutrow called IEAH co-president Michael Iavarone after the colt worked that morning at the Palm Meadows Training Center in Boynton Beach, Florida, and told him, "You're not going to believe this, but I want to enter him right now."

Even though Dutrow's original plan had been to keep Big Brown on the grass and then run in the Blue Grass Stakes at Keeneland, on the synthetic Polytrack, he saw little downside in taking a shot when the Gulfstream allowance race was switched to the dirt on race day because of rain.

"If I had not been there that morning he worked before that allowance race, I would have not entered him, but what I saw was that he could beat horses in a one-other-than. I saw that. So, I say to myself, 'Who is he going to hook in an a-other-than at Gulfstream?' I'd been watching the horses in the stakes, and I knew he could beat them. So who is going to show up in a one-other-than? So what's the big deal; he gets a little bit tired, but he is still going to beat these horses. I'm saying all this stuff to myself. And if we don't run him, and keep training him, we are going to miss out. So we took a shot. It was an unbelievable feel-ing that day. Unbelievable."

Immediately after the allowance race, Dutrow bowed out of the trip he was going to take to Dubai to saddle two horses on the Dubai World Cup undercard—the IEAH-owned Benny the Bull in the $2 million Dubai Golden Shaheen, and Diamond Stripes, who was owned by Kassem Masri's Four Roses Thoroughbreds, in the $1 million Godolphin Mile. Those races were scheduled for March 29, the same day as the $1 million Florida Derby.

"I had my tickets to Dubai; I was going there with Diamond Stripes and 'Benny,' and I was happy to do it," he said. "But when Big Brown took control of that allowance race turning for home, and by the time he was galloping out, I told Iavarone, 'There is no way I'm going to Dubai. I'm staying here with this horse.'"

Big Brown capped an amazing day for Dutrow by winning the Florida Derby in front-running fashion by five lengths. Earlier in the day, Benny the Bull and Diamond Stripes, who were saddled by Michelle Nevin—Big Brown's exercise rider and Dutrow's assistant—were winners in Dubai.

The Florida Derby was Big Brown's final Kentucky Derby prep. The five weeks between the Florida Derby and Kentucky Derby fit Dutrow's preferred spacing of races for the stakes horses in his barn.

The lead-up to the big race in Louisville was a heady time for Dutrow, who was tickled with the eager manner in which Big Brown approached his training at Palm Meadows following the Florida Derby.

"The last day he trained at Palm Meadows, he was the only horse on the track and he was surrounded by three ponies," Dutrow said. "He walked to the track with the three ponies. He did his little thing and the three ponies were there waiting for him afterward. It was the funniest, coolest scene. Then throughout the morning, I was just waiting there at the barn with him to jump on a plane with him to go to Kentucky. It was crazy. It just was a feeling I've never had before. It was just unbelievable to know you were going to take him to Kentucky to run in the Kentucky Derby. It was very exciting."

Like Curlin the year before, Big Brown was a horse who had

everyone talking. No one questioned their talent; both were striking physical specimens who had displayed astonishing raw power, yet both lacked the seasoning that was usually necessary to win the Derby. Both had made only three starts going into the longest, most demanding test of their brief careers. Even Curlin, who had gone on to be named Horse of the Year, could only manage to finish third in Louisville.

Nevertheless, Big Brown was sent off as the 2-1 favorite, and justified that price, and his trainer's faith, by cruising to a 4¾-length victory.

Dutrow, the trainer who had once waited seven years for his first winner, didn't even give himself time to savor winning the most famous race in America before setting his sights on the next prize. Even months later, he said that he was still not sure it had all sunk in.

"I didn't even think about it then. I didn't sit there and think, 'We won the Derby.' Nothing like that happened. After the Derby, I was only interested in the Preakness. We did a big dinner Derby night and it was beautiful, but I was only interested in the Preakness. And after the Preakness, how could I be interested in anything else but the Belmont?"

On a sweltering June afternoon, Big Brown went to the post at Belmont as the 1-4 favorite, with a crowd of 94,476 expecting to see a coronation. Instead, Big Brown was eased on the far turn and was pulled up, finishing last.

"After the Belmont, I was: 'What the hell is going on? Something must have happened.' Everything changed. Then it was: 'What is up now? I got to get this horse right. Something has got to be wrong for him to be pulled up in a race.'"

The strange outcome of the Belmont Stakes was right out of a Dick Francis mystery, except for the fact that nothing sinister happened to Big Brown. Back at his barn, where a horde of media flocked after the debacle, Big Brown was walking soundly and had no apparent injuries. Dutrow informed the assembled press that he didn't have an explanation for the stunning defeat.

Meanwhile, in the interview room in the basement of the Belmont Park grandstand, jockey Desormeaux stated, "This horse was in no way, shape, or form lame or sore, but there's something amiss. He's probably just tired and I thought in this horse's best interests, let's just get him back to the barn and recharge his batteries."

In the days that followed, theories abounded. Horse racing is all about differences of opinion, and everyone had one, from the local deli guy to the most seasoned turf writer. Was the culprit the wired-together quarter crack on Big Brown's left front hoof that surfaced a week after the Preakness and kept him from training for three days? Was it the absence of the monthly injection of Winstrol, which Dutrow said he elected not to give to Big Brown before he ran in the Belmont, but was administered before the Derby and Preakness? Did his left hind shoe, which photographs showed to be dislodged during the running of the race, cause Big Brown discomfort? Was it the extreme heat and humidity on that June afternoon? Or did Big Brown lose energy after becoming uptight in the pre-race monitoring barn?

Four months after the Belmont flop, Dutrow stood by what he told *Daily Racing Form* reporter David Grening two days after the race, which was that Desormeaux's ride leaving the gate and going into the first turn of the Belmont Stakes, Big Brown's only loss during his eight-race career, was hardly textbook.

"I don't know what happened to Big Brown in that race," Dutrow said in September 2008. "I know the first half-mile of the race had a whole lot to do with it."

The trainer had anticipated that Big Brown, a horse with natural speed, would be in front after breaking from the rail in the Belmont. Instead it was 38-1 shot Da' Tara, the eventual gate-to-wire winner, who secured the early lead. Big Brown's head was cocked slightly to the inside while his body drifted to the right leaving the gate, and Desormeaux would say later that starter Roy Williamson, who was standing on the track to spring open the gate, as he customarily does, may have startled his mount.

Desormeaux and Big Brown found themselves on the heels of Da' Tara and jockey Alan Garcia going into the first turn. Then they were in a box among three horses: Macho Again, Anak Nakal, and Tale of Ekati. To extricate himself from the crowding, Desormeaux tugged on Big Brown to maneuver him into the clear. Big Brown bumped with Anak Nakal before locating a free lane outside Tale of Ekati. Meanwhile, Da' Tara, who wasn't part of the fray, had surged to a three-length lead around the first turn.

"I didn't see anything happen when he straightened away going down the backside to the wire; nothing got in his way then," Dutrow recalled. "I'm never going to know. I can only be led to believe that the first half-mile of that race messed him up.

"If you want to say it was the starting-gate guy in Big Brown's way and he was shying from him; if you want to say it was the back shoe; if you want to say it was too hot in the monitoring barn before the race—anybody can say whatever they want— but there is no way of me ever knowing. I have been with this horse night and day, and I know I didn't see anything wrong with the horse. So, I don't know.

"By the time I was walking back through the tunnel, I could see the horse was fine. The only thing I did see was an issue with his back shoe, but he walked fine and when my blacksmith went to take it off, he didn't flinch away from it and he walked off perfect. No way anybody is going to tell me the back shoe cost him that race. Kent said he felt smooth as silk in the race. If Kent said there was something wrong behind and you take off the back shoe and see him flinch and he walks off funny . . . But, that didn't happen. Hundred percent every minute, the horse was after the race."

In September 2008, Dutrow said that Desormeaux was not his pick to be partnered with Big Brown; that call was made by Iavarone, who tabbed the Hall of Fame jockey as Big Brown's rider for the Triple Crown shortly after IEAH bought into the colt.

It wasn't difficult to figure out who Dutrow would have preferred to have aboard Big Brown when he offered this: "[Edgar] Prado fits a horse like a glove; he just lets them alone," he said of the rider he uses often. "A jockey is supposed to be [a passenger]. You break out of the gate; sometimes they break good, sometimes they don't. If they don't, now you're playing catch-up. Maybe you have a speed horse that wants to be in front and he doesn't break that good and some horse gets in his path and you're in trouble. It might be the jock's fault the horse doesn't break good; or it might not be. It's a tough call. I like to ride riders who just leave horses alone. Prado is excellent at that. I like things to unfold naturally."

Dutrow said if he had it to do all over again, he would not change anything in Big Brown's preparation for the Belmont Stakes. Two days after the Preakness, Big Brown was shipped to trainer Bobby Frankel's barn at Belmont Park and took up residence in the stall that was once occupied by the Frankel-trained Empire Maker, the 2003 Belmont Stakes winner. Dutrow, whose New York stable is based at Aqueduct, wanted Big Brown to train on Belmont's main track in preparation for the third leg of the Triple Crown, and since Dutrow and Frankel are friends, it was a logical stabling arrangement.

"Big Brown trained the way we wanted for the Belmont," he said. "After the Preakness, I told everyone that all we needed was one breeze; basic stuff. I know I didn't do anything wrong with Big Brown from the Preakness to the Belmont, and I have Frankel to verify that. He was there every day with the horse because we were in his barn at Belmont. Frankel saw the horse, just like I did. He told me, 'Rick, you've done a great job.'"

Dutrow got Big Brown back on course after the Belmont dud. The colt returned to take the Haskell Invitational at Monmouth Park on August 3, then won an ungraded turf race, the Monmouth Stakes, on September 13, which was meant to be Big Brown's prep for a much-anticipated matchup with reigning Horse of the Year Curlin in the Breeders' Cup Classic at Santa Anita October 25. But on October 13, while breezing on the turf at his Aqueduct home base, Big Brown injured himself when his right hind leg struck the inside of his right front foot, ripping off a chunk of flesh. Less than two hours later, Iavarone announced the colt's retirement. Big Brown entered stud in 2009 at Three Chimneys Farm in Versailles, Kentucky.

It was a sad day for Dutrow and his staff when Big Brown left. Dutrow becomes very attached to his horses and he considers them his friends. He said he prefers the company of his horses over most people. If you walk into Dutrow's barn at any time during the day, you might find him hugging his horses and talking to them. Visitors are usually offered peppermints to feed the horses and are encouraged to take a stroll around the barn unaccompanied for a meet-and-greet with the horses. Like a proud parent, Dutrow is wont to say, "Babe, you've got to see Benny [the Bull]; he's down there. He looks fantastic."

One of Dutrow's favorite horses was Saint Liam, who was

owned by William and Suzanne Warren. The Saint Ballado colt came into Dutrow's barn during the summer of his 3-year-old campaign in 2003. At that point, Saint Liam had won two races in eight starts. Saint Liam, who was plagued with brittle feet and quarter cracks throughout his career, really blossomed at 4 and 5. Dutrow said the transformation in Saint Liam's temperament, which took place while under his care, was primarily the reason that the horse finally realized his full potential.

"When Saint Liam came to us, he was as mean as a snake," Dutrow said. "You would not want to be around him. He would want to hurt you and as time went by, and we put all those issues to rest, he became a sweetheart—so nice to be around. There is a picture of him and Molly at Saratoga and they are just hugging each other. That never would have happened when he first came to us; he would rip you apart. You put the trust in him, and man, he just loved living with us. After we got him running, it took a year and a half before he was completely into his life. It took a while."

In his first two starts for Dutrow, Saint Liam easily won back-to-back allowance races, first at Aqueduct in December 2003 and then at Gulfstream Park the following month. Saint Liam's 4-year-old campaign included a win in the Grade 2 Clark Handicap at Churchill Downs and in-the-money finishes in the Grade 1 Woodward, in which he was second to eventual Horse of the Year Ghostzapper, the Grade 2 New Orleans Handicap (second), and the Grade 2 Oaklawn Handicap (third).

As a 5-year-old, Saint Liam won the Grade 1 Stephen Foster Handicap, was second in the Grade 1 Whitney Handicap, and won both the Grade 1 Woodward and Breeders' Cup Classic at Belmont Park. He was retired after the Breeders' Cup and won Eclipse Awards as Horse of the Year and champion older male.

The $4 million Classic represents the richest race won by

Dutrow. To further sweeten the trainer's bonanza on October 29, 2005—which also included winning the $1 million Sprint with Silver Train—he wagered $160,000 to win on Saint Liam, who was the Classic's 2-1 favorite, and made $384,000.

It's not unusual for Dutrow to wager large amounts on his horses, but he said the bet on Saint Liam was his biggest plunge.

"That's by far the most I've ever bet," Dutrow said. "I've bet $50,000 [to win] a few different times. But with Saint Liam, I felt we had so much the best horse in the field. He was running on a track he loved and had a good post [12]."

Dutrow was asked when he knew he had a top horse in Saint Liam, and his face lit up at the recollection.

"When he won his three-other-than at Gulfstream, I knew we had a runner," he said. "I knew he was a good one at the three-eighths pole in that race. I didn't know until then. That's when we went for the gut. We went right after the big boys after that. We went right to the New Orleans Handicap. And the horses in that race might have been the toughest he ever ran against. You had Ten Most Wanted. You had Peace Rules. You had Funny Cide. Saint Liam went off at 6-1 in the race. That was a tough race."

Saint Liam, who was ridden by Edgar Prado, finished second in the New Orleans Handicap to Peace Rules, who was ridden by Jerry Bailey. The margin of victory was a head, and the outcome generated plenty of controversy after the stewards took no action against Peace Rules, who exchanged bumps with Saint Liam during a rousing stretch duel.

"Saint Liam was the best horse that day," Dutrow said. "The stewards should have put Saint Liam up. I can't believe they didn't. [But] we didn't cry or complain."

Early in Dutrow's career, he primarily operated a claiming operation. Some of those claimers turned into stakes horses, including Sis City, whom Dutrow cites as his best claim. Acquired for $50,000 out of a winning effort in a maiden race for 2-year-olds, the filly became a multiple stakes winner and earned $795,764. Among her victories for Stonerside Stable and Diamond Pride LLC were the Grade 1 Ashland and Grade 2 Demoiselle.

Dutrow said she had good speed figures, so he "took a shot."

"She was very sound and pretty straightforward. What she really needed was two turns and she got that."

When claiming, Dutrow approaches the process in this manner: "I'm a horse-for-a-course kind of guy," he said. "So at the fall Belmont meet, I'm looking for horses who might like the inner track at Aqueduct because that is coming up later. I'm not going to be looking at horses that run big at Belmont and run big at Saratoga and don't show up at the inner track. So you are looking for the future when you claim a horse. If I get this horse, I ask myself, 'What am I going to do with this horse? Where am I going with this horse?' So you got to claim for their future by seeing their background."

One of the things Dutrow looks for in a potential claim is sluggishness out of the starting gate. That is not a bugaboo for Dutrow; in fact, he lists that as one of the reasons he might be drawn to a horse. He theorizes some runners break poorly because of hind-end issues, which often are fixable.

"If anyone can straighten them up, we can," he said. "That is where their power is. That's where they are pushing off. If they break sluggish five out of 10 times in the past performances, we are going to look into that. We've always had a vet that is good with hind-end issues."

Dutrow said the most important role a vet plays in his barn is the evaluation of horses' hindquarters.

"When my horses are messed up behind it is important for me

to have someone to fix them," Dutrow said. "Anything other than that, I don't think is it important to have a top veterinarian. I think I can handle most of everything else. I know what is happening up front with horses. If something starts going wrong with their breathing, a basic vet should be able to scope them and see the trouble.

"But the hind end is different. It's hard for me to see what is wrong with them behind. I certainly couldn't fix it because I wouldn't know if it is their hocks, stifles, glutes, back leg suspensory . . . There are so many different things; it's not my game. But I do know when they are not right behind. And I will try to fix them up until we get them right because that is where their power is. And they have to be straightened out behind. If you don't have a horse whose hind end is right, you can't have that full horse on your side. You are giving [something] away, and I hate to do that."

At one time Dutrow used the services of the prominent veterinarian Dr. Steven Allday, whom the trainer described as "the best that I have seen with hind-end issues." Two of Dutrow's charges who benefited from Allday's work were Stalwart Member and Classic Endeavor. Both had been stakes winners before coming into Dutrow's barn, but their form had tailed off before he claimed them. Three and a half months after Classic Endeavor was taken by Dutrow for $50,000 in August 2004, he won back-to-back starts in the Stuyvesant and Queens County Handicaps and then finished third in the $1 million Sunshine Millions Classic. One month after Stalwart Member was claimed for $35,000 by Dutrow in July 2000, the gelding won back-to-back allowance races and followed with wins in the Grade 3 Sport Page—the trainer's first victory in a graded race—and the Hudson Handicap.

Around 2006, Dutrow and Allday had a public falling-out, and the trainer no longer uses the vet. Allday said Dutrow "didn't play by the rules" in a 2008 *Boston Globe* article. Dutrow's response is that Allday "is a nut."

Another strategy Dutrow employs when making claims is assessing the abilities of other trainers. If he senses that a horse isn't reaching his or her potential in another trainer's barn, and he believes he can do a better job with that horse, he will swoop in for the claim.

"There are trainers out there who we think are complete clowns, so you've got to be interested in claiming off of them," he said. "I don't want to name any names. But they know who they are, and so do we."

With the proliferation of quality stock filling his stalls, Dutrow, who had about 100 horses in his stable in 2008, doesn't claim in the hand-over-fist fashion he once did. But old habits die hard, and he often finds himself perusing past performances for a claimer ripe for the taking.

"I do miss the claiming a little bit, I do," he said. "I try to get myself interested in claiming from time to time as I am looking through the paper. I ask myself, 'Do I want this horse in my barn?' I then get not so excited about it. I don't know, I ain't got nothing against the claimers, but I want to get exciting horses in the stable. But at the same time, when my people call me and want to claim, I'm not going to say no. I like my people and I want to keep them as happy as I can.

"There are certain trainers I won't claim from, and it is building up more and more. That's another reason I'm not so interested in claiming anymore. I won't claim off guys I have a relationship with. It's mostly the good guys in the game," he said, reeling off a string of names: Allen and Jimmy Jerkens, Bill Mott, Todd Pletcher, and Kiaran McLaughlin. "Those kind of guys, I would never claim from them. . . . I like these guys, and we get along good. It takes away from the claiming game because they are dropping them in to win, and I'm not there to take them because I don't claim from those guys."

One of Dutrow's trademarks is running horses back on short rest, although he doesn't do that as often with the higher-class and stakes horses in the barn. It's not uncommon for him to race a horse, and on that same day, even before the race is run, enter the horse to run three days from then.

"If I have a horse that wins by four or five and he is looking good and there is a proper spot for him, three, four, five days from then, he is going to run that same race back the same way," Dutrow said. "He's still in that zone that he was in. It works. I don't know why, and I don't care why. And I'm not going to look into why; I just know that it works. So I'm going to keep doing it as long as my horses get the proper spot in three, four, or five days.

"I don't like doing it so much in the hot weather because it takes a lot out of them. In the winter, I'll do it all the time. It's just [taking advantage] of the situation when it comes up. It's just the racing game. It's just something I do. I can't tell you that I copied from somebody. It's just me watching my horses run, and seeing one that I think is a good one to run back quickly. I just listen, watch, follow, and do it.

"I don't like doing it with the good ones," he added. "I don't usually do that. The ones I do it with are the claiming types or maybe an allowance horse where you know they are not going to develop into being a good one. I don't want to do it with a good horse, but I have, and it hasn't worked out so well with the good ones."

Dutrow's philosophy on breezing horses boils down to where they are in their training and when they will run next. As an example, Dutrow mentioned Big Brown, who was being prepared for the Breeders' Cup Classic when he answered the question regarding his approach to workouts.

"In their breezes, I look for them to be well within themselves and the riders to come back and tell me how happy they are with the horse," Dutrow said. "If that doesn't happen, then I have to look into the horse to get the horse to breeze well within himself and be happy doing it. That's what I am looking for with the breezes. Like with Big Brown right now, I don't know that I am going to tell Michelle [Nevin] that we need to get a really good work into the horse from now to the Breeders' Cup. I think it should all be basic stuff; nothing special to it because Big Brown has been running and we know how good he is and we don't need to find out again in the morning.

"I don't like when my horses breeze fast, unless they are coming off a six- or seven-month break and I have plenty of time to get them ready. Then maybe I would ask them for a little bit of run two breezes before they run. It has a lot to do with the situation. If you have a horse whose knees are bugging him and know you are going to run him, I'm just looking for a nice, basic breeze. I don't know if you can categorize the breezes. I think with each horse, each breeze has to be the way you want them to go for the situation that is coming on. I don't think you can say, 'I just want all mine to breeze a particular way.' I think the best way to train horses is to treat them like individuals, as opposed to treating them all the same."

No matter what Dutrow has already achieved or the good work he will most likely do in the future, suspicion will surround him because of his medication violations and his extraordinary 25 percent career win rate.

Dutrow isn't losing any sleep over what people think of him or his operation.

"All people need to do is to come into my barn and see how

RICK DUTROW

VITAL STATISTICS

CATEGORY	STS.	W%	ROI
1stNAStart	3	0	0
1stAfterClm	39	0.26	1.73
2ndAfterClm	29	0.31	1.76
1stRaceTrn	81	0.31	2.19
180+Trn	47	0.15	1
61-180Trn	77	0.23	1.43
2nd45-180Lay	93	0.29	1.64
2nd180+Lay	34	0.18	0.96
1-7Last	44	0.25	1.98
1stStart	49	0.12	1.05
2ndMdn	45	0.31	2.82
MSWtoMCL	20	0.3	2.04
1stTurf	19	0	0
1stBlink	15	0.2	2.41
1stLasix	12	0.58	4.94
2YO	63	0.22	1.46
Dirt/Turf	34	0.21	1.05
Turf/Dirt	41	0.37	4.45
BlinkOn	16	0.25	2.69
Sprint/Route	88	0.24	1.63
Route/Sprint	78	0.24	2.29
Sprint2/Route	18	0.28	1.85
31-60Days	300	0.23	1.65
WonLast	169	0.31	2.32
Wet	117	0.22	1.18
Dirt	591	0.26	1.9
Turf	164	0.19	1.5
Sprints	411	0.23	1.69
Routes	350	0.25	1.92
MCL	85	0.31	2.18
MSW	72	0.21	1.17
Claim	259	0.23	1.49
ALW	165	0.24	1.62
STK	137	0.25	2.68
GSTK	46	0.26	3.36
DebutMCL	20	0.15	1.74
Debut>=1Mile	8	0.12	0.71
Synth	6	0	0
Turf/Synth	2	0	0
Synth/Turf	3	0	0

*January 1, 2008, through February 8, 2009, North American runners only

CAREER HIGHLIGHTS

BREEDERS' CUP

STARTS	1ST	2ND	3RD
10	3	1	0

WINNERS
Saint Liam: Classic (2005)
Silver Train: Sprint (2005)
Kip Deville: Mile (2007)

TRIPLE CROWN

STARTS	1ST	2ND	3RD
3	2	0	0

WINNERS
Big Brown: Kentucky Derby, Preakness (2008)

ECLIPSE AWARDS
Saint Liam: Horse of the Year (2005);
  Older Male (2005)
Benny the Bull: Sprinter (2008)
Big Brown: 3-Year-Old Colt (2008)

RECORDS/NOTABLE ACHIEVEMENTS
Leading trainer in New York in 2001, 2002, and 2005.

Reached 1,000 career wins with Kip Deville on March 3, 2007, in the Frank E. Kilroe at Santa Anita Park.

CAREER SUMMARY

STS.	1ST	2ND	3RD	EARNINGS
5,350	1,337	949	774	$64,074,331

*Through February 8, 2009, North American runners only

we do things," he said. "We do all the basic stuff the right way. We take care of our horses. With us it's all about the horse. There is not even a question mark about that. Put them in the right spots. It's simple to me. I feel good about what I do. If someone thinks I am doing something that you are not allowed to, I don't care what they think. I'm doing good, man."

Three

Bobby Frankel

Imagine the career path that would lead to becoming one of the world's most successful Thoroughbred trainers, and the ideal route might look something like this: Grow up in the heart of horse country, somewhere in Kentucky or Maryland, England or Ireland. Make your way to the racetrack at an early age and hook up with a well-respected trainer, working your way from hotwalker to groom to assistant, or possibly top exercise rider. Spend years in a master-apprentice relationship, learning everything you can about the centuries-old craft of conditioning racehorses, until at last you branch out on your own with a handful of clients, courtesy of your former mentor.

Or, if you're Bobby Frankel, just dive in.

"I worked three months as a hotwalker for a guy named Buddy Bellow," Frankel said. "That was it. Then I went out on my own."

Within a few years he was already known on the New York circuit as the King of the Claimers. These days he lives in Pacific Palisades, California, and trains for a Saudi Arabian prince.

Frankel was born July 9, 1941, in Brooklyn, New York. He was the younger of two sons of Gertrude and Merrill Frankel, caterers and owners of a toy store. Gertrude passed away while Frankel was in his 30s; Merrill died in 1991.

"They were good people, you know," Frankel said. "They took good care of us. They were honest, hardworking people."

Until Frankel was 8 years old, his family lived in Brooklyn. They later moved to Far Rockaway, not far from Aqueduct, where he saddled his first winner, Double Dash, in 1966.

Frankel's parents enjoyed going to the races, and often brought him along.

"My parents first took me to Roosevelt Raceway, and then my father took me to Belmont one day," he recalled. "My mother and I would go to the races a lot together. We took the ferry to Monmouth. We also would go up to Saratoga. She was a good handicapper."

Frankel vividly remembers the biggest score of his youth, which took place at Aqueduct.

"I made a lot of money one day before I was training, when I was in my late teens," he said. "I bet on a horse ridden by Bobby Ussery, my favorite rider. He won six races that day. I walked into the track with $40 and I walked out of there with $20,000. I bet a $20 double on two favorites. The double paid $14, so now I have $140 bucks, plus the other $20, so I have $160. Ussery won the third, fourth, fifth, sixth, and seventh. He got beat in the feature and was second. I loved the winner that day in that race, too. Ussery came back and won the last race. One of the horses I bet that Ussery rode paid 30 bucks, so I had some serious money there to gamble. I came home and put the money on my mother's bed and she thought I robbed a bank. At that time, I don't think my father was making $20,000 a year."

By his own admission, Frankel was a terrible student because the inclination wasn't there. He barely managed a semester at C. W. Post on Long Island before quitting and heading back to the racetrack, where he continued to gamble before deciding at the age of 25 that he would become a trainer. After his win with Double Dash, one of Frankel's next winners was Pink Rose, a horse he bought for himself.

"I bought my first horse off Allen Jerkens for $8,500; that's why I always have a soft spot in my heart for Allen," Frankel said. "She was a Hobeau [Farm] horse, Pink Rose, and I ran her at Aqueduct in 1966. I ran her for $12,500 first time out and she got beat a head. I ran her back, and she didn't run good. And then I ran her back for $6,500 at Saratoga, and she won, and she won again and again—all claiming races.

"I didn't have a clue as to what I was doing. Allen had her good and sound, and she would lay up there close to the pace. Then I got her good and sore, so she dropped back."

Frankel is self-deprecating as he recalls his early days as a trainer, but eight years into his career, when he was 33 years old and knocking them dead on Southern California's racing circuit, he wasn't shy about letting everyone know how good he was. In a 1974 *Sports Illustrated* article, he stated, "I definitely think I'm the best trainer in the business. I'm not scared of any other trainer alive."

When Frankel was shown the *Sports Illustrated* article in the fall of 2008, he chuckled and said, "I was a cocky bastard, wasn't I?"

He might have been young and brash, which didn't endear him to the more seasoned trainers he was competing against, but Frankel earned his bragging rights. Coping with the myriad physical problems that plague claiming horses—basically the bread and butter of his stable for the first 15 years he was in the business—was no easy feat.

"I walked around my barn the other day looking at my 36 horses and trying to count the really sound ones," he told the writer of that 1974 *SI* article. "I counted up to one."

But Frankel's years as a handicapper had honed his instincts about which horses would make good claims, and where they could be spotted in order to win. In 1967, his second year of training, he won only nine races from 101 starts, but the next year he was up to 36 winners from 165 starts. One of his more successful maneuvers was taking Barometer for $15,000 and turning him into the winner of the 1970 Suburban Handicap, a race that had been won by great horses such as Assault, Tom Fool, Nashua, Bold Ruler, Kelso, Buckpasser, and Dr. Fager. The same year, Frankel shared the Saratoga training title with Jim Maloney.

He moved to Southern California in 1972, and for more than 20 years, he made Del Mar, Hollywood Park, and Santa Anita Park his primary bases of operation. Training titles came in rapid succession. Frankel won a record 60 races at the Hollywood Park meet in 1972; eight more titles followed there. Seven titles were secured at Santa Anita's Oak Tree meet, and another five at Santa Anita's winter meet. At Del Mar, he earned five training titles.

All those achievements, which took place from 1972 through 1982, were largely accomplished with claimers. If a horse was sore or had foot problems, he would call on the services of blacksmiths and veterinarians, and he took the time to analyze each runner individually, trying to figure out how to get the maximum result.

"There's not just one way to train a horse," he said in *Sports*

Illustrated. "There's six or seven different ways. And who knows which one will work best? Especially since a horse is different from day to day. This has got to be the biggest guessing game ever invented. . . .

"What I try to do is bring a horse up to a race at some kind of peak of soundness and as fit as possible under the circumstances. You have to compromise. If you try to get the horse too fit, by working him a lot, he may never make it to the race at all.

"But that's where the guessing game comes in again. Nobody knows where the peaks are; every trainer has his own idea of how fit you can get a horse while still keeping him sound. You've just got to keep trying, and it isn't easy, especially when you're on top. Being a leading trainer is a lot of pressure; it's tough. And the hell of it is that even if you guess right, everything you do amounts to maybe half a length; that's about all. But one little mistake can cost you thousands of dollars."

In the 1980s, Frankel's barn received a boost with an influx of quality horses from clients that included prominent owners Bert and Diana Firestone; Edmund Gann, who would team with Frankel to win the 1988 Japan Cup with Pay the Butler and campaign millionaire Al Mamoon; Stavros Niarchos, a powerful international presence who had owned the great Nureyev and was the leading owner in France in 1983 and 1984; and record executive Jerry Moss, who would win graded stakes with Frankel-trained runners such as Ruhlmann, Garthorn, Fighting Fit, and Sharannpour. Frankel also trained Mehmet, who twice upset reigning Horse of the Year John Henry in 1982, winning the Carleton F. Burke on turf at Santa Anita and the Meadowlands Cup on dirt.

Frankel said there was no magic surrounding his transition from a trainer of claimers to stakes horses.

"It wasn't hard," he said. "You are around other trainers and you see how they train. It's an open book out there. You just have to be realistic and do the best you can. Treat the horses really well."

A pivotal point in Frankel's career came in 1990, when he began a most lucrative association with Prince Khalid Abdullah of Saudi Arabia. Abdullah's far-flung racing empire had been a prolific presence around the world since he started Juddmonte Farms in 1977, but Frankel wasn't completely aware of how powerful an operation it was until he started training Abdullah's beautifully bred horses.

Out of the blue, Frankel received a phone call in 1990 from Abdullah's North American racing manager, Dr. John Chandler.

"Dr. Chandler asked if I would like to train for them," Frankel said. "I'd seen the name but didn't realize how really big they were. A friend of mine was training for them at the time, Eddie Gregson, and I just didn't feel like taking the horses from him. So I said, 'Eddie is a friend of mine, can I let you know tomorrow?' So, I asked Eddie, and he said, 'Listen, I'm going to get fired anyways. It's a great outfit, you should take the job.' Juddmonte was surprised I didn't jump on it and take the job right away."

Frankel started training a few horses for Juddmonte and did well with them. In 1991, Juddmonte sent him Exbourne, and Frankel was absolutely smitten with the horse that came with plenty of baggage from Europe.

"I would say one of my biggest accomplishments came with Exbourne," Frankel said. "They had this horse in Europe and they couldn't get him to the races. Grant Pritchard-Gordon, their racing manager at the time in Europe, called me up and said, 'We've got this really nice horse.' He had been laid up for like 18 months or something. They said I could try him, but not to worry about it if he doesn't make it. I did real well with him.

He was a top, top-class horse; a beautiful horse but such a cripple.

"If I had Exbourne today, I probably couldn't get him to the races because I was a little more aggressive back then, and when they were sore, I went on with them," he added. "Nowadays, I might have backed off a horse as sore as him. I remember that I felt guilty that I went on with him because he was sore, but if I didn't go on with him, he never would have been the horse he was."

Exbourne, a turf runner, retired to the breeding shed with earnings of $999,989, and wins in the Hollywood Turf Handicap, Caesars International, Shoemaker Handicap, and Eddie Read Handicap.

Frankel's connection with Juddmonte continued to flourish in the 1990s, with Wandesta (1996) and Ryafan (1997) earning titles as champion turf female. In 2005, Intercontinental added another championship in that division off her victory in the Breeders' Cup Filly and Mare Turf, becoming the first Breeders' Cup winner that Frankel saddled for Juddmonte. They won their second Breeders' Cup together in 2008 with Ventura in the Filly and Mare Sprint.

The list of stakes winners trained by Frankel for Juddmonte is extensive: Aptitude, Beat Hill, Cacique, Chiselling, Defensive Play, Empire Maker, Flute, Heat Haze, Honest Lady, Indian Flare, Latent Heat, Light Jig, Marquetry, Price Tag, Quest for Fame, Raintrap, Sightseek, Tates Creek, Tinners Way, and War Zone.

"It's the greatest job, working for Juddmonte," said Frankel, who had 20 horses for Abdullah in his care in 2008. "You feel real secure, and it's not like you are under the gun all the time. They don't overplay their horses, thinking they are the greatest horses in the world when they send them to you. A lot of people will send you horses, and even before they breeze they are telling you they are Grade 1 horses. Plus, Juddmonte got me to the point where other big outfits took notice."

Those big outfits Frankel referred to are Stronach Stable, whose principle, Frank Stronach, is the chairman of Magna Entertainment, the largest major racetrack operator in North America, and Bob and Janice McNair, the proprietors of Stonerside Stables. In the fall of 2008, the McNairs sold the majority of their racing and breeding assets to Sheikh Mohammed bin Rashid al-Maktoum's Darley Stable. The McNairs employed several trainers, and in the immediate aftermath of the sale to Darley, the horses in training remained with their current trainers, although changes in the lineup of trainers did come later.

Frankel, who was inducted into the Hall of Fame in 1995, said in Abdullah, Stronach, and the McNairs, he found owners who encouraged his patient approach to training.

"They're the three easiest owners I have," he said in June 2008. "They like to take their time, like I like to do. If I run a horse too much, they will tell me, 'Let's freshen him up a bit.' The horses I really think I do better with are the horses that need a little time, and don't want to be run at five furlongs in May or June. Horses that develop as you go along—those are the types of horses my big outfits send me."

When the quality and number of horses in his stable began to burgeon in the late 1990s, Frankel decided to open another division in New York, and since 1999 has been a regular fixture at Belmont and Saratoga. In 2008, between his New York and California divisions, he had a total of 100 horses.

"I have to do it," Frankel said, referring to maintaining a presence on both coasts. "I want to stay in California. I have a beautiful home there, and I love California. But if I kept them in

California they would be running against each other all the time. The upside is that I really like training on the tracks back east. For the horses, I think it is better."

Frankel has a plethora of grass runners in his stable, so he might have been expected to jump on the bandwagon with those extolling the virtues of synthetic racing surfaces when California law issued a mandate that synthetics would replace the conventional dirt surfaces at all the state's Thoroughbred tracks in 2007. It is widely believed that turf form generally translates well to synthetic surfaces, and indeed, the Frankel-trained Ventura, who began her career on grass and Polytrack in England, took to the brand-new Pro-Ride surface at Santa Anita by winning the 2008 Filly and Mare Sprint by four lengths over the previous year's champion 2-year-old filly, Indian Blessing.

Nevertheless, Frankel sees the pros and cons of synthetic surfaces.

"They need a lot of maintenance. You get different injuries. I don't think it's any safer than the grass," he said. "The only edge you got on synthetics is that when it rains, you don't get a sloppy racetrack. That's what I like about it. You got New York and Churchill Downs that haven't changed to synthetics, and I don't think they should change. I'll tell you one thing: I think synthetic tracks are going to change the breed around with more breeders breeding for that surface."

For the most part, Frankel trains his grass horses on the main track, especially if the turf course is getting chewed up at the end of a meet. But at Belmont Park, Frankel does send some of his grass runners to the turf course in the morning because he said the composition of the main track is so sandy and deep that turf horses have difficulty maintaining their footing over it. Overall, he believes racing on the turf is more forgiving, but noted that any surface has the inherent potential for injuries.

"I think you get more bowed tendons with grass horses than dirt horses, because they slide more on grass; at least that's my theory," he said. "That's why I think they get tendons on sloppy racetracks, too."

When a young horse arrives in Frankel's barn with a pedigree that indicates it will be better suited to one surface than another, he reserves judgment until he assesses the horse.

"I go with an open mind," Frankel said. "I remember a case where I entered a horse on the turf, and the owner told me that out of his first three dams, there was not one grass winner. He ended up a winner on the turf."

Keeping an open mind and taking time with each horse do not seem like attributes that fit the former "cocky bastard" who pushed hard to get sore runners to the races and proclaimed that he was the best trainer in the country, but perhaps time and the inevitable disappointments have mellowed Frankel. He says he is his own worst critic. He doesn't take losing well. At the end of a bad day, he will go home placing the blame on his shoulders, particularly if he believes he could have managed a situation better. And sometimes, he realizes there are cases where horses just get beat, through no fault of his own. But he still finds any loss difficult to stomach.

"There have been a lot of disappointments—a few Breeders' Cup disappointments," Frankel said. At one point, racing's showcase day was a source of angst for the trainer, who was 0 for 38 in Cup races before notching his first win with Squirtle Squirt in the 2001 Sprint at Belmont Park.

"I don't know how confident I really am going into any race," he added. "You always think you can train them a little differently. The longer I am around, I think the less confident I am every time I run a horse. You see so many things go wrong. You love so many horses you think couldn't lose, and they lose. I'm hard on myself when I think I should have done better with a horse and I haven't. And I don't need anybody to tell me because I'm thinking about it all the time."

Frankel may be haunted by his losses, but for him the true nightmare is when a horse loses its life.

"Every time you lose one, I really feel terrible," he said. "I'll never forget Phantom Rose, a filly out of Honest Lady, who came from Europe and just ran off the television screen and set a track record at Hollywood Park. She was difficult to train.

"I took her up to the training track and put a pair of blinkers on her. When she came around the turn, she bolted. And the outside rail at Hollywood Park's training track was wrought iron, and had no give in it whatsoever, and boom, she hit it with her rear end and broke her leg and we had to put her down. I was there and saw it happen. I felt so guilty about that; you know how things go on in your mind afterward? You wonder what you could have done differently. Those things are really hard for me."

Since Squirtle Squirt, Frankel has saddled five more Breeders' Cup winners, perhaps most notably Ghostzapper, who provided Frankel with his first Classic win in 2004 at Lone Star Park. Ghostzapper, who was owned by Frank Stronach, became the first Frankel-trained runner to earn a Horse of the Year title, and was also named champion older male.

Because he trains mostly for breeders, Frankel rarely, if at all, buys horses at auction.

"I'm not really a student of pedigrees," he said. "I'm happy to take what I am given."

One bloodline Frankel is particularly familiar with, and fond of, is that of Toussaud, whom he trained to win the 1993 Gamely Handicap, a Grade 1 at Hollywood Park, for Juddmonte. Toussaud's offspring included four Grade 1 winners, all trained by Frankel: Chester House, the winner of the 2000 Arlington Million; Chiselling; Honest Lady, who earned nearly $900,000; and 2003 Belmont Stakes winner Empire Maker.

Toussaud, the 2002 Broodmare of the Year in the United States, had plenty of quirks, and she passed her idiosyncrasies on to some of her foals. A daughter of El Gran Senor, Toussaud wasn't malicious, according to Frankel, but just strong-willed, and did things as she pleased, not at the beckoning of those around her.

"Toussaud was the most difficult horse I ever trained," he said. "We used to jog her the wrong way in the mornings and she would stop and throw her head. She busted the nose of one of my exercise riders. And then you had to work her from the gate with other horses just to get her to go."

Frankel had no idea what to expect from the progeny of Toussaud, who died in 2009. What he discovered was that they were difficult to manage, but the payoff came in the form of brilliance on the racetrack.

"I think horses like that are more intelligent than the other horses," Frankel said. "They are leaders instead of followers. They weren't mean horses by any means. They were all sweet horses. I had one I couldn't train at all—Civilisation. He pulled up in the middle of a race. He was a half-brother to Empire Maker."

Empire Maker provided Frankel with his first win in a Triple Crown event—but not the one that the trainer coveted most, and expected to win. Empire Maker, winner of the Florida Derby and the Wood Memorial, was the clear favorite for the 2003 Kentucky Derby, and Frankel had every reason to be hopeful that the son of 1990 Derby winner Unbridled would fill one of the few gaps in his resume.

Frankel, who was on a stakes-winning roll that had resulted in

Eclipse Awards as the country's leading trainer for three years in a row, had started four horses in the Derby in previous years, with runner-up Aptitude giving him his best finish in 2000. He summed up the significance of winning the Derby by telling Jay Privman of *Daily Racing Form*, "You can win the Pacific Classic six times, but no one knows who you are. People in the business do, but not anyone else. What am I going to say when people ask if I've won the Derby? I finished second?"

When Empire Maker bruised a foot and missed a day of training leading up to the Derby, Frankel remained confident, telling Rich Rosenblatt of the Associated Press, "Bet against him at your own risk," but on race day, the colt did lack his usual knockout punch and finished second behind Funny Cide, whom he had beaten in the Wood.

Empire Maker skipped the Preakness so Frankel would have a fresh horse for the Belmont, and in his absence, Funny Cide, a New York-bred gelding, romped by 9¾ lengths and came into the Belmont gunning for a Triple Crown sweep in front of a hometown crowd. Empire Maker played the spoiler in the Belmont, overpowering Funny Cide in the sloppy going to win by three-quarters of a length over Ten Most Wanted, with Funny Cide finishing third.

"This is probably the biggest thrill in racing for me," Frankel later told Beth Harris of the Associated Press. "A little redemption here."

As for depriving racing fans of the chance to witness a long-awaited Triple Crown victory by a popular horse who was consistently portrayed as the plucky underdog with Average Joe connections, Frankel said, "I haven't walked in the streets yet to see what happens with the people," but added, "At least I'm from New York, and the horse is named Empire Maker, like the Empire State Building."

Following the Belmont, Empire Maker made what would turn out to be his final start in the Jim Dandy at Saratoga. After finishing second in the Jim Dandy, a subsequent injury prevented the colt from continuing his 3-year-old campaign, and Juddmonte ultimately decided to retire him in the fall of 2003. He was sent to stud at Juddmonte's Kentucky-based farm. Empire Maker's first crop of runners hit the track in 2007. His initial graded stakes winners included Acoma and Mushka, and the Frankel-trained Country Star.

"Empire Maker was just a really good horse," Frankel said. "He was a little difficult to train. He was okay at the beginning, then he picked up some of his mother's traits. Luckily, knock on wood, I haven't had any trouble with any of Empire Maker's foals. I was really apprehensive how they would be. I had been a little worried, but the foals are straightforward. They have all been good. And I believe Empire Maker is going to have some classic horses."

Before Empire Maker came along, the trainer was primarily known for his deft touch with grass horses. Although Empire Maker proved there was no labeling Frankel's talent, he continued to excel with turf runners. One of those was Leroidesanimaux, a South American import owned by Stud T N T and Stonewall Farms Stallions. The Brazilian-bred horse, whose name means "the king of the animals," appropriately won the 2005 Eclipse Award as champion turf male.

"I've been lucky with South American horses," Frankel said. "My record is pretty good with them. I think the key is they just need a little more time because they are coming from a different hemisphere. Most of the horses they send me are young; and they are six months behind in age [compared to North American-foaled horses]."

Another of Frankel's successful South American imports was

Lido Palace, a multiple Grade 1 winner in 1997, and during the summer of 2008 the trainer privately purchased Vineyard Haven, a 2-year-old colt by that stallion. After the sale, Vineyard Haven was campaigned by Frankel in partnership with Los Angeles Dodgers manager Joe Torre and Louis Lazzinnaro. Vineyard Haven provided the trainer with his first win in the Hopeful Stakes at Saratoga. Frankel said it was the first time he recalled starting a 2-year-old colt in a Grade 1 race. Vineyard Haven followed his Hopeful score with an ultra-impressive winning performance in the Grade 1 Champagne. The colt was not nominated to the Breeders' Cup, and Frankel decided to pass on the Breeders' Cup Juvenile, primarily, he said, because he wanted a fresh horse for the 2009 Triple Crown.

In the days before the 2008 Breeders' Cup at Santa Anita, Frankel was asked what he expected to see from Vineyard Haven when the colt turned 3 years old. The trainer got a wistful look in his eyes, and said, "I tell you, he's a good one."

What he didn't say, however, was that he had already been approached by the Maktoum family to buy Vineyard Haven. About a week after the Breeders' Cup, Frankel announced that Vineyard Haven had been sold for an undisclosed price to the Maktoums' Godolphin racing stable.

When the deal was sealed, Frankel said it was bittersweet to let Vineyard Haven go, but in the end, his business acumen overrode any misgivings he had regarding the sale of a top 3-year-old prospect.

"I couldn't refuse the offer; I had to let him go," Frankel said. "I had already turned down two offers before, and I finally let him go. This is one of the best horses I have trained. He was good to me, so sure I will root for him. How could I not?"

A perk for Frankel is that some of his top runners continue to give after they have been retired. Frankel, who owns about a half-dozen mares, said he has free breeding rights to Empire Maker, Ghostzapper, Medaglia d'Oro, Aldebaran, Peace Rules, Mizzen Mast, and Midas Eyes. He sells some of the breeding seasons because he doesn't have enough mares to take advantage of them.

Mizzen Mast, a Grade 1 winner for Juddmonte and Frankel, is the sire of Mast Track, with whom Frankel won the 2008 Hollywood Gold Cup as the breeder, trainer, and owner. Mast Track's dam, Nawal, was trained by Frankel and raced by Edmund Gann. Frankel acquired Nawal after the completion of her racing career.

Frankel said it means a great deal to him that he has managed the careers of many horses who have become successful sires or broodmares—and he doesn't believe this has happened by chance.

"I don't know why, but I have a theory: because none of them have had steroids. The Ghostzappers, the Empire Makers, the Mizzen Masts, none of them had steroids. The mares that went back to Juddmonte Farm, they never had steroids."

In 2008, the use of anabolic steroids in Thoroughbreds became a heated topic in the racing industry and in Washington, D.C., where a congressional hearing was held. Racing regulators have since adopted new rules concerning the use of steroids, and their presence in a horse's system on race day is now illegal in most racing jurisdictions. According to Frankel, it will have little if any impact upon his operation.

"Over the years, I've probably used steroids in less than 100 horses; maybe in 50 horses," Frankel said. "I don't think in the last year I've given a steroid to a horse."

He added that it's common to hear stories about claiming horses moving up with the use of steroids. "And that's bullshit. I claimed a million horses and I never gave them steroids."

Through 2008, Frankel's runners had amassed earnings of $219,994,950, placing him only behind D. Wayne Lukas, who led the all-time earnings list in North America with $251,513,535. During this decade, his stable has consistently struck at a 20 percent win rate or higher. In 2004, Frankel reached the winner's circle with a whopping 28 percent of his runners.

Asked how he would respond to those who believe those numbers can't be achieved without using illegal medications, Frankel said, "Just look at the horses and the owners I have got, and then judge off of that. It's not like my horses are paying $50, or their form just completely changes. The better horses you get, the better your percentages are going to be. If you get a crop of horses that aren't talented, your percentage is not going to be as good."

One of the luxuries of having those "better horses" is that they tend to stay around longer, as opposed to the claimers who came and went in Frankel's earlier days, and it is his custom to become attached to his runners. Some of his notable favorites over the years were Flute, Ginger Punch, Happyanunoit, and Sightseek. Happyanunoit was a Grade 1 winner in 1999, 2000, and 2001; Flute won the 2001 Alabama and the Kentucky Oaks; Ginger Punch captured the 2007 Breeders' Cup Distaff en route to a championship title; and Sightseek was a multiple Grade 1 winner and earner of $2.4 million.

Happyanunoit and Ginger Punch were so cherished by Frankel that he named two of his beloved Australian shepherds after the fillies. When Happy, Frankel's dog, was losing her battle with lymphoma in the fall of 2007, he didn't want to leave her side to travel to New Jersey for the Breeders' Cup at Monmouth Park. So Frankel watched Ginger Punch win the Distaff on television from California. A few months later, in honor of his fifth Breeders' Cup winner, Frankel acquired another Australian shepherd and named her Ginger.

Sightseek isn't exactly a name that would work well for a pet, but Frankel probably gave it some consideration because he was very, very fond of the filly. A Juddmonte homebred, Sightseek won seven Grade 1 races during the course of 2003 and 2004. She had credentials that in most years would have been good enough to win back-to-back Eclipse Awards. Sightseek was the winner of the 2004 Ruffian, Beldame, and Ogden Phipps, which followed her victories in the 2003 Beldame, Go for Wand, Ogden Phipps, and Humana Distaff. Sightseek, however, had the misfortune of going up against the mighty Azeri in the voting for the divisional title in 2003 and 2004, and was the runner-up on both occasions.

Frankel became emotional in the winner's circle following Sightseek's final career start in the 2004 Beldame at Belmont Park. At the time, he said, "This is definitely the best mare I've trained on dirt." While acknowledging that "The Eclipse Award is up to the voters," he was nevertheless unable to resist pointing out in the next breath that Sightseek had beaten Azeri by 11 lengths in the Ogden Phipps, while Azeri beat her by a length and three-quarters in the Go for Wand. "I know Azeri is the darling of everybody, but this is a great filly," he said.

Four years after that final race, Frankel lit up at the mention of Sightseek, whose first foal, an Empire Maker filly named Striking Example, was born in 2006. He was anticipating her arrival in his barn in 2009.

"Sightseek was a big strong filly, but so sweet that she wouldn't hurt a fly," Frankel said. "She didn't have a mean bone in her body. But she was a really difficult horse to ride in her races. She was rank. I think if she was an easier horse to ride, she never would have gotten beaten. She was her own worst enemy because her first step out of the gate was slow and the field would leave her. After about 50 yards, she would jump into the bridle and she would get rank."

One of Frankel's favorite riders was Sightseek's regular pilot, Hall of Famer Jerry Bailey, who retired in 2006. Bailey rode a multitude of Grade 1 winners for Frankel, including Empire Maker, Flute, Medaglia d'Oro, Peace Rules, and Squirtle Squirt.

"I was lucky with Bailey," Frankel said. "The thing I respect most about him was that he came to the race so well-prepared. He knew the speed. He would come to the paddock and before I would open my mouth, he would lay the race out for me in 30 seconds."

Frankel's favorite Bailey ride came in the 2002 Test Stakes at Saratoga aboard You. The Frankel filly brought a glitzy resume to the Test with wins earlier that year in the Acorn, Santa Anita Oaks, and Las Virgenes, as well as victories in the previous year's Frizette and Adirondack. Among You's opponents in the Test was the undefeated Carson Hollow. The Test unfolded with Carson Hollow establishing a sizzling pace, while You lingered in last place down the backstretch of the seven-furlong race. Bailey moved You into contention through a microscopic hole on the rail in the stretch, and a stirring battle ensued between You and Carson Hollow. As the fillies streaked under the finish line, track announcer Tom Durkin roared, "A photo finish that doesn't deserve a loser!" You won the photo.

"That was probably one of the greatest top 10 races of all time," Frankel said. "Jerry rushes up the inside and gets through a hole that wasn't there. Bumped a horse out of the way, got through. From the three-sixteenths pole to the wire, You and Carson Hollow were so close together. I couldn't tell who was in front. Their heads weren't bobbing; they were going simultaneously. I think the reason I won was because You had a big, long head on her."

Carson Hollow was trained by Rick Dutrow Jr., who is a friend of Frankel's. When Dutrow won the Kentucky Derby and Preakness with Big Brown in 2008 and was aiming for a sweep of the Triple Crown, he opted to train the colt at Belmont Park rather than at his Aqueduct home base. Dutrow asked Frankel if Big Brown could stay in his barn, and Frankel was glad to oblige.

While the hordes of media covering the Belmont Stakes were corralled into a secured area outside Frankel's barn, Dutrow and Frankel were often visible as they sat on lawn chairs outside the barn talking out of earshot of the journalists.

Frankel said he did give Dutrow advice on how to handle the media crush, but laughed and said he thought he had failed because Dutrow gave some flippant answers anyway and offended several of his peers by proclaiming that their horses had no chance against Big Brown in the Belmont.

"Keep your mouth shut, you know," Frankel said in reference to Dutrow's boasting. "Hey, I'm friends with him. He's not a bad guy, but he just needs to learn to keep his mouth shut. The press is looking for stuff like that. Just look at the [New York] *Post* every day. The press loves him. I'm the opposite, I try to avoid and stay away from the press. Rick shouldn't have been talking so much about Big Brown. There's always time after the race to brag all you want. And it's just as effective. If you brag before the race, it's bad vibes."

Interviewing the laid-back Dutrow, who responds to questions in freewheeling fashion, is an experience in stark contrast to conducting an interview with Frankel. If you don't come prepared with a question that Frankel considers worth his time to answer, you will be met with a taciturn or even gruff response.

Frankel's take on reporters: "There are some I trust, and some people I wouldn't say things in front of."

When it comes to television interviews, getting Frankel to commit is no easy feat. Good luck to the person from the network assigned to lure Frankel on the air before a race. If someone is fortunate enough to persuade him, viewers should not expect to glean much from the interview.

"What is gained by being interviewed before the race?" Frankel said. "I say, 'The horse is doing great.' Every trainer says that. Then when they run like shit, you look like an idiot. You're in a no-win situation. After you win, you're happy and you can brag and talk all you want. If you say before a race, you really don't think you have a chance and the horse wins, people are going to get pissed off at you. I haven't heard too many trainers telling the press, 'This horse has got that wrong with him.' You're just going to hear how great a horse is doing. So what does the public learn from that?"

Frankel says his most significant achievement is the world record he established for saddling the most Grade 1 winners in one season, which he set in 2003 with 25 wins. It was nearly eclipsed in 2008 by the European-based Aidan O'Brien, who fell just three Group 1 victories short of snatching the record from Frankel.

"What an unbelievable run," Frankel said with a huge smile on his face. "That is my biggest accomplishment and the one I am most proud of."

The year 2003 also marked the season Frankel led the nation in money won ($19,143,289), which shattered the previous record of $17,842,358, set by Lukas in 1987. Frankel also added a record fifth Eclipse Award training title to his cache that year.

Several longtime key staff members in the Frankel barn were part of that record-setting season. Humberto Ascanio, with

Frankel since 1973, is his California-based assistant. Rubin Loza, with Frankel since 1977, shares that role in New York with Jose Cuevas, who also gallops for Frankel.

Frankel said he demands plenty from his staff. When something goes awry in the barn, they will hear about the transgression immediately, and probably not in a mild-mannered fashion. But Frankel is very fond of Ascanio, Cuevas, and Loza, and honored them in a touching and special way by inviting each of the men to the stage when he won his fourth Eclipse Award in 2004. He cited each of the assistants during his acceptance speech.

"I will be tough on them," Frankel said. "I'm not easy. I get frustrated when they make mistakes or things aren't going right. But I don't hold grudges. [Problems] are settled, and then it's over with. I think some of these guys have been around for so long because I take care of them. I treat them good. I pay them good."

Cuevas, who came to New York as Frankel's assistant in 1999 with seven horses, was asked one morning at Saratoga what it was like to work for Frankel. He was at a loss for words—perhaps because his boss was standing nearby.

"How can I put it?" Cuevas pondered. "How can I put it, Bobby?"

Frankel ignored the question. Instead, he asked Cuevas why some grooms were walking his horses to the monitoring barn without bandages.

Cuevas patiently said, "Because the vets have to check the horses as soon as they get there."

Frankel watched a group of horses from another stable make their way to the monitoring barn. "What do they have to check? Those guys are walking over there with bandages."

Frankel wasn't done yet. "Is that filly over there already?"
Cuevas: "Yes."

BOBBY FRANKEL

VITAL STATISTICS

CATEGORY	STS.	W%	ROI
1stNAStart	19	0.21	1.33
1stRaceTrn	30	0.17	0.98
180+Trn	38	0.16	0.85
61-180Trn	102	0.2	1.8
2nd45-180Lay	84	0.23	1.54
2nd180+Lay	18	0.17	0.61
1-7Last	2	0	0
1stStart	37	0.05	0.62
2ndMdn	38	0.13	1
MSWtoMCL	12	0.25	2.52
1stTurf	40	0.12	0.86
1stBlink	21	0.14	1.31
1stLasix	22	0.23	1.33
2YO	12	0.25	3.3
Dirt/Turf	24	0.21	1.69
Turf/Dirt	72	0.18	2.03
BlinkOn	25	0.16	2.05
BlinkOff	13	0.23	1.3
Sprint/Route	66	0.14	1.12
Route/Sprint	57	0.21	1.34
Sprint2/Route	14	0.21	1.9
31-60Days	196	0.2	1.72
WonLast	107	0.22	1.74
Wet	23	0.3	1.99
Dirt	98	0.3	2.23
Turf	285	0.17	1.16
Sprints	199	0.18	1.39
Routes	336	0.18	1.43
MCL	29	0.21	1.66
MSW	143	0.1	0.86
Claim	39	0.1	0.74
ALW	161	0.24	1.55
STK	161	0.2	1.85
GSTK	139	0.2	1.88
DebutMCL	1	0	0
Debut>=1Mile	8	0	0
Synth	152	0.13	1.35
Turf/Synth	51	0.2	2.17
Synth/Turf	45	0.16	0.83

*January 1, 2008, through February 8, 2009, North American runners only

CAREER HIGHLIGHTS

BREEDERS' CUP

STARTS	1ST	2ND	3RD
79	6	9	8

WINNERS
Squirtle Squirt: Sprint (2001)
Starine: Filly and Mare Turf (2002)
Ghostzapper: Classic (2004)
Intercontinental: Filly and Mare Turf (2005)
Ginger Punch: Distaff (2007)
Ventura: Filly and Mare Sprint (2008))

TRIPLE CROWN

STARTS	1ST	2ND	3RD
16	1	4	1

WINNERS
Empire Maker: Belmont (2003)

ECLIPSE AWARDS

Leading Trainer (1993, 2000-03)
Bertrando: Older Male (1993)
Possibly Perfect: Female Turf Horse (1995)
Wandesta: Female Turf Horse (1996)
Ryafan: Female Turf Horse (1997)
Squirtle Squirt: Sprinter (2001)
Aldebaran: Sprinter (2004)
Ghostzapper: Horse of the Year (2004);
  Older Male (2004)
Leroidesanimaux: Male Turf Horse (2005)
Ginger Punch: Older Filly or Mare (2007)

RECORDS/NOTABLE ACHIEVEMENTS

Inducted into racing Hall of Fame, 1995.

Won a record fifth Eclipse Award as leading trainer in 2003.

Won a world-record 24 Grade 1 races in 2004.

Set a Santa Anita record for career wins at that track (900) in 2008.

Was the nation's leading money-winning trainer four times (1993, 2001-03).

All-time leading trainer at Hollywood Park.

Reached 3,000 career wins with Megahertz in the 2004 San Gorgonio Handicap at Santa Anita Park.

CAREER SUMMARY

STS.	1ST	2ND	3RD	EARNINGS
17,426	3,619	2,959	2,465	$222,211,365

*Through February 8, 2009, North American runners only

"Is someone over there with her?" Frankel asked and when given an affirmative response, continued his questioning. "What guy?"

"Bobby, the same guy that goes over there with every horse, every day," Cuevas said with a hint of exasperation in his voice.

Cuevas then smiled wryly, as if to say, "Here's your answer to what it's like to work for him."

Four

Neil Howard

For racing historians, 1984 will be best remembered for the inaugural running of the Breeders' Cup at Hollywood Park. Also making headlines that year was the news that Kentucky Derby winner Swale had collapsed and died of an apparent heart attack just eight days after winning the Belmont Stakes, while on a happier note, the popular 9-year-old gelding John Henry became the first horse to capture the Arlington Million twice.

The fact that owner William S. Farish of Lane's End Farm tabbed the relatively unknown Neil Howard as his private trainer didn't attract much notice in 1984. While they might have started quietly, however, Farish and Howard have built a successful and headline-worthy relationship, which saw its silver anniversary in 2008.

Howard was 35 when he became head trainer for Farish, the founder of legendary Lane's End Farm, which covers

2,000 rambling acres in Versailles, Kentucky. Lane's End, established in 1979, is one of the preeminent breeding operations in the world, producing homebreds that carry its own colors on the racetrack, as well as candidates for the auction ring.

At first glance, Farish and Howard seemed an unlikely coupling.

Howard, who grew up in Riverdale, New York, a middle-class section of the Bronx, had no family connection to racing and was the son of a glassblower. His father, who died when his only child was young, owned a small shop in the Bronx that specialized in making thermometers for cargo-ship refrigerators.

But if you didn't know about Howard's urban upbringing, you might even mistake him for a native Kentuckian. Any trace of a New York accent is long gone.

"I always felt out of place [in New York]," Howard said. "It's weird. I never wanted to be there. I guess sometimes there are things brewing inside a person and you act on them when you can."

Howard began riding at a stable near his home when he was a kid. Later, his work with hunters and jumpers led him to the racetrack, where he sought Thoroughbreds who couldn't cut it as racehorses but might prove useful as show horses. In the late 1960s, his travels took him to Waterford Park, now known as Mountaineer Casino Racetrack, in West Virginia. Howard said he immediately "fell in love with the racetrack, and at Waterford Park, no less."

Following a two-year stint in the navy, when he was stationed in Norfolk, Virginia, and in Cuba, Howard got his first job at the track as a groom with trainer John Cotter at Belmont Park.

Farish, born in 1939 in Houston, Texas, has deep roots in racing. He is the grandson of oil magnate William Stamps Farish II, who established one of the 20th century's most prolific racing and breeding operations, Lazy F Ranch. When he died, his legacy was continued by his wife, Libbie Rice Farish, and his daughter, Martha Gerry. Gerry, who died in September 2007 at the age of 88, campaigned three-time Horse of the Year Forego, was one of the first three women to be elected to The Jockey Club, and was the first woman to be named an Exemplar of Racing at the National Museum of Racing in Saratoga.

Will Farish's late father-in-law, Bayard Sharp, was an owner and breeder, and it was with Sharp that Farish first became actively involved in racing as an owner in 1963. Nine years later, he notched his first classic win with Bee Bee Bee in the Preakness, upsetting 2-year-old champion and Kentucky Derby winner Riva Ridge.

As Farish's racing and breeding operation continued to gain strength, Howard's racing career was launching quietly in Ohio. He saddled his first winner, Knock Knock Bird, at River Downs in 1979, and scored his first stakes victory the next year with Hasty Tam, who took Beulah Park's Ohio Open Championship Handicap.

Before he became a trainer, Howard had forged what would turn out to be a very important friendship with Mike Cline, whom he met when they both worked for Hall of Fame trainer Mack Miller in New York. Cline, now the farm manager at Lane's End Farm, held that position in 1982, the year that Farish's private trainer of 12 years, Del Carroll Sr., died of head injuries after falling from Farish's colt Sportin' Life during a training accident at Keeneland.

Cline put in a good word for Howard with Farish, and Howard left Ohio in 1982 to work at Lane's End, moving to Kentucky with his wife, Sue, whom he had met on the racetrack when she was galloping horses. Howard spent one breeding season at Lane's End, acquiring an education working with broodmares and foals. The next year, he accompanied the Lane's End yearlings to Camden, South Carolina, where they received their early schooling. In 1984, Farish was satisfied that he had found the right person to replace Carroll, and Howard accepted the offer on a handshake agreement.

Howard identifies his stable as "midsize for today's climate." He keeps about 25 horses in his barn while racing at Keeneland and Churchill Downs in the spring, summer, and fall, and at Fair Grounds in the winter. Another 15 to 20 horses who are either being freshened, coming back from injuries, or are backward 2-year-olds remain at Keeneland's annex training facility year-round. Howard said he "takes what fits" to Saratoga's six-week boutique meet.

Today, private training jobs are an anomaly. Family-owned breeding operations such as Calumet Farm, Elmendorf Farm, Greentree Stable, and Rokeby Stable are now something for historians to write about and longtime racing fans to remember nostalgically. Of course, the Phipps family and Jack Dreyfus's Hobeau Farm continue to operate stables with Hall of Fame trainers Shug McGaughey and Allen Jerkens, respectively, but the emergence of popular and successful racing syndicates such as Dogwood Stables, IEAH Stables, Team Valor, and West Point Thoroughbreds has changed the face of the game tremendously.

Typically, the syndicate ownership groups carry a large number of horses, and spread their wealth of horseflesh among more than one trainer. Even Farish has a small division in Canada with trainer Mark Casse to take advantage of the lucrative purses that have resulted from the windfall of the slots operation at Woodbine.

Perhaps what is truly remarkable about Howard and Farish's association is that it has withstood the test of time, and has done so in a business where trainers are frequently fired and replaced by the latest hotshot on the block.

Howard is cognizant of his good fortune. He said one of the reasons his arrangement with Farish works is that his boss does not berate him when things go wrong in the stable.

"I'm extremely fortunate," he said. "I take every day like it is my first day on the job. I make my mistakes, but Mr. Farish is not a dweller. If I drop the ball, we'll talk about it that night, or right afterward we'll discuss it. It might be brought up the next day, but rarely. He knows me and I know him. He knows what it takes and how hard it is. Our goals are not always met. He can watch a race and know when things go wrong. He knows when we are barking up the wrong tree, and sometimes he knows quicker than I do, and I appreciate that input, believe me.

"He has that uncanny way of when something gets screwed up he will ask me anything but that. That means so much to me. I know damn well he has the right to be aggravated. He is human, but I appreciate the fact he will talk about everything but that. That takes a certain type of person. There are not many people around like that. He reminds me of Paul Mellon a lot," Howard said, referring to the late founder of Rokeby Stable.

During the eight years in the 1970s that Howard worked for Mellon's private trainer, Mack Miller, rising through the ranks from groom to foreman, he had a bird's-eye view of the inner workings of the private-trainer position. When Howard first arrived in Miller's barn, his boss was training for Charles Engelhard Jr.'s Cragwood Stable. Later, Miller became Mellon's principle trainer, a job that lasted for 18 years until Miller retired at age 74, an event that coincided with the 88-year-old Mellon's dispersal of his horses.

During the time Howard worked with Miller, he had no inkling he would land one of those coveted private training positions, but he said his observations of Miller's association with Engelhard and Mellon prepared him well for his future role.

"It was interesting," Howard said. "I didn't realize at the time how fortunate I was to see how Mack Miller interacted with Mr. Mellon, and also with Mr. Engelhard. I feel like that helped me now."

Noting that private jobs are few and far between these days, he added, "When you are given the opportunity to do what you love and have a free ride to do it, maybe there is an extra couple of degrees of respect that you show these people. You want to do the best you can do at the highest level possible. I saw that between Mr. Miller and Mr. Mellon and Mr. Engelhard."

Howard's reverence for his employer extends as far as never addressing Farish and his wife, Sarah, as anything other than Mr. and Mrs. Farish.

"It's funny, you know, because if you held a gun to my head, I couldn't see myself calling them Will and Sarah. One of the reasons I do it is because I feel it is the proper thing to do, and I never want to miss an opportunity to show my respect to the Farishes. I think that is one way of doing it."

Respect is one thing, but delivering the goods is another. Howard has delivered for Farish, who often breeds and races horses in partnerships. Stakes winners developed by Howard for Farish solely or for partnerships include Summer Squall, Runup the Colors, Secret Status, Lil's Lad, Shadow Cast, Midway Road, Quick Tip, Rock Slide, Alumni Hall, Reunited, and Grasshopper. But there is no question that the most accomplished horse Howard has trained for Farish was Mineshaft, the Horse of the Year and champion older male of 2003.

If matters had worked out according to their original plan, Howard might not have trained Mineshaft, who was co-bred and co-owned by Farish and the late James Elkins Jr. and W. T. Webber Jr.

Mineshaft began his racing career in England as a 3-year-old in April 2002, under the care of trainer John Gosden. The primary reason Mineshaft was sent to England was because Farish was going there in August 2001 to serve a 3½-year stint as the U.S. ambassador to Great Britain and Northern Ireland, a position he was nominated for by former President George W. Bush. Farish has been a friend to the Bush family for several decades.

Farish was fond of Mineshaft from the time his mating was planned because the colt represents everything brilliant about Lane's End. Farish co-bred and co-owned A.P. Indy, Mineshaft's sire and the 1992 Horse of the Year and 3-year-old champion. Farish and William Kilroy bred A.P. Indy, and the Lane's End consignee was the highest-priced yearling of 1990, selling for $2.9 million at Keeneland in July. He was bought by Tomonori Tsurumaki, who sent A.P. Indy to trainer Neil Drysdale in California. Farish and Kilroy, in partnership with Harold Goodman, later bought into A.P. Indy following his win in the 1992 Belmont Stakes. After A.P. Indy's victory in the 1992 Breeders' Cup Classic at Gulfstream Park, the colt was sent home to Lane's End, where he developed into one of the world's leading sires.

The same year that A.P. Indy was making a splash as a 3-year-old, Mineshaft's dam, Prospectors Delite, a Farish homebred, won the Grade 1 Acorn for her breeder and Howard.

So it was no surprise that Farish wanted to keep close tabs on Mineshaft while he fulfilled his duties as ambassador in England.

"Mineshaft was a unique situation; he was immature early," Farish said. "But there was something about him that really appealed, to the degree that I sent him to England with me when I served as ambassador. John Gosden trained him on the all-weather track at Manton, and he trained exceptionally well. As I said, he was immature, so we didn't run him until 3. We saw he didn't handle the gallops over soft going particularly well, but when you put him on the all-weather track, you saw just tremendous potential. John said, 'I think he is an exceptional horse, but I think he needs to be back in America because he is never going to realize his potential on the soft going.' If we had a summer in England where the ground was firmer, it might have been a different story, but that wasn't the case. So we took him back to Neil early in the fall of his 3-year-old year. Neil saw right away what Gosden said. And he really began to blossom at Churchill on the dirt."

By the time Mineshaft left Gosden, he had won just once in seven turf starts, and placed third in the Group 3 Prix Daphnis at Maisons-Laffitte in France. But the real Mineshaft quickly revealed himself upon arrival at Howard's Churchill barn in the fall of 2002.

Mineshaft won a one-mile allowance race on the dirt at Churchill by 1½ lengths as the favorite on November 27. He followed with another handy allowance score on December 20 at Fair Grounds. That day, he steamrolled eight rivals by 3¼ lengths, and earned the comment "charged gate" from *Daily Racing Form*'s chart caller.

"When I got the horse, he was a baked cake," Howard said. "I communicated with John Gosden, and he said, 'Just do your thing.' He was an uncomplicated horse. I'll never forget when I got him in the barn that fall. From day one, he acted liked he had been there his whole life. He went to the racetrack like nothing to it."

Mineshaft won his first start of his 4-year-old season in the listed Diplomat Way Handicap at Fair Grounds on January 19, then ran back 22 days later in the Grade 3 Whirlaway Handicap at the New Orleans track and finished second by 2½ lengths to an accomplished stakes horse, Balto Star. The Whirlaway loss was still a solid effort from Mineshaft, who earned a 107 Beyer Speed Figure.

Racing on the anti-bleeding medication Lasix for the first time, Mineshaft was sent off at odds of 5-1 when he ran next in the Grade 2 New Orleans Handicap on March 2. Ridden by Robby Albarado, who was his partner in his 11 American starts, Mineshaft motored to the lead around the far turn and drew off to win by 3½ lengths over 10 rivals. His time of 1:48.92 for the 1⅛ miles was strong, and good for a 116 Beyer.

After Mineshaft whipped an overmatched field of three rivals by nine lengths in Keeneland's Grade 3 Ben Ali in April, the time had arrived for Farish and Howard to target the country's major handicap races. Mineshaft would earn his first Grade 1 in the Pimlico Special when he splashed through the slop en route to a 3¾-length victory on May 16.

Up until that point, there hadn't been the slightest hitch in Mineshaft's training. But things got a bit hairy for Howard in the days leading up to the Grade 1 Stephen Foster at Churchill Downs, run four weeks after the Pimlico Special.

Howard had received a heads-up from Gosden that Mineshaft had delicate feet, something he had inherited from A.P. Indy, who was scratched from the 1992 Kentucky Derby on the morning of the race due to a quarter crack.

"John warned me that Mineshaft had weak [hoof] walls," Howard said. "We put on glue-on shoes, so as not to insult the feet with nails. It worked beautifully and we had the glue-on shoes through the winter. But we couldn't leave them on constantly."

Howard said they shod A.P. Indy with regular shoes five or six days before the Stephen Foster. "The next morning, he walked out of the stall, giving it the Frankenstein. I said, 'I have to call Mr. Farish right now.' I looked at my watch; I didn't care what time it was in England. I called him, and said, 'We've got a little bit of a problem here.' On Monday we took the nail-on ones off, and went with the glue-ons. Right away, he was a little better, but it took two or three days. That was the only race he didn't come up to perfect, but I thought he was okay to run."

Mineshaft's issues with his feet, or perhaps what some observers perceived as an overconfident ride by Albarado, resulted in a neck loss to the gritty gelding Perfect Drift in the Stephen Foster. Albarado moved on Mineshaft heading into the far turn, and the colt quickly spurted to an open-length lead. Perfect Drift, under patient Pat Day, gained momentum on his rival in the stretch and wore down the 7-10 favorite in the final strides.

Howard said Mineshaft bounced out of the race in perfect shape, and the trainer was eager to tackle the Grade 1 Suburban Handicap at Belmont Park on July 5. He had no qualms about running Mineshaft back in three weeks, but Farish was a bit wary.

The discussion Howard and Farish had regarding the Suburban illustrates the ease at which they arrive at decisions mutually.

"After the Stephen Foster, Mr. Farish expressed concern about running him back three weeks later in the Suburban," Howard said. "I told Mr. Farish I thought the problem was [a result of the] feet situation. No more, no less. He said, 'Okay, I'm with you.' If I feel strong, he will go along with me."

Farish said the reason he and Howard clicked from the start was that they share many of the same viewpoints.

"He had a horseman's background when he came to me," Farish said. "And you know, a lot of times what makes something like this work is the synergy between two people. After a year working for me on the farm, I knew that his ability as a horseman and outlook on training would fit our philosophy.

"I don't think in all the years, Neil and I have had major differences of opinion. Ultimately, I will always prevail." Farish paused, laughed, and said, "I'm kidding about that. We just sit down and reason together about it. We try to figure out the best way to do something. Do we take the horse to New York and prep or do we take an easier route? Decisions have always been based on the horse: What is best for the horse."

The decision to run in the Suburban paid off. Making his first dirt start at 10 furlongs, Mineshaft looked like a luxury car in cruise mode as he motored past the previous year's Breeders' Cup Classic winner, Volponi, and won by 2¼ lengths.

Mineshaft received a freshening after the Suburban in anticipation of a fall campaign. Already the leading contender for the titles of Horse of the Year and champion older male, he reasserted his dominance with breathtaking wins in the Grade 1 Woodward and Grade 1 Jockey Club Gold Cup at Belmont Park during a three-week span in September.

The great run ended in the Gold Cup. Six days later, the Mineshaft camp announced the colt's retirement to Lane's End Farm for a stud fee of $100,000. Howard and his veterinarian, Foster Northrop, said in a national telephone conference on October 3, 2003, that a small nondisplaced chip in Mineshaft's right front ankle was discovered after he won the Suburban in July. Their comments after the Gold Cup were the first public acknowledgment of the injury.

Following the Gold Cup, Mineshaft was returned to Kentucky, where Howard said X-rays revealed that the chip had broken free and was "floating" in the ankle joint, which made racing him risky.

Despite ending his career before the Breeders' Cup, which has become a major factor in crowning champions, Mineshaft was the runaway winner in the Eclipse Award ballots for Horse of the Year and older male.

Mineshaft retired with earnings of $2,283,402 and a record of 10-3-1 from 18 starts. His first crop of 2-year-olds reached the races in 2007.

"I don't know if I will see another horse like that, but in my position there is the chance to because I'm very fortunate to get these well-bred horses every year," Howard said. "Having had a horse like Mineshaft was a twofold gratification for me. It meant everything to my career. I also felt that with a horse like him, in some ways, I was able to give back a little bit. In other words, I am never going to fully pay back Mr. Farish and his family for what they have done for me, and that is truly how I feel. But to have Mineshaft come back to Lane's End to stand, I don't think there is anything more gratifying to a breeder and a farm owner. It's like sending a horse off to kindergarten, and then sending him home four years later, as a potential leading stallion."

Howard's other big horse was Summer Squall, a Farish-bred son of Storm Bird out of Weekend Surprise, the dam of A.P. Indy. Farish sold Summer Squall as a yearling at Keeneland for $300,000, and he was bought by Cot Campbell's Dogwood Stable, a racing syndicate. Campbell, the president of Dogwood, then sold 40 shares in Summer Squall, and Farish was one of 28 investors. With Farish's approval, Dogwood sent Summer Squall to Howard.

Summer Squall, the runner-up to Unbridled in the 1990 Kentucky Derby, provided Howard with his first and only classic win in the Preakness. The colt had scored victories as a 2-year-old in the Hopeful, Saratoga Special, Bashford Manor, and Kentucky Budweiser Breeders' Cup, and concluded the that it gives him a handle on the family traits of runners he has trained, and what to be on the lookout for in their offspring. A good example of that was Secret Status, an A.P. Indy filly who provided Howard and Farish with their first Kentucky Oaks win in 2000.

"Secret Status was an extremely talented filly, but a very nervous filly," Howard said. "I always told Mr. Farish I wish we knew then what we know now about GastroGard and some of the top-quality medicines that we didn't have then for ulcers. I'm pretty sure now [ulcers] caused a lot of her problems. Her offspring are not necessarily nervous because we have more things to help them now. Case in point: You get something out of being on the lookout for something you noticed earlier, because you know the potential is there with the family."

Knowing the quirks of a family also aids Howard in determining a training program for a horse.

"My first approach to training is to go by what the individual horse needs, but I do have a leg up on the majority of the horses I get because I know the family, and sometimes I use the same training methods with their offspring," he said.

"What works is not getting away from the basics. The smaller and light horses don't need a strong training program as much as some of the colts do. A horse like Mineshaft, you just needed to stay out of his way because he was a very honest horse in his training. If you wanted him to work a half in 50 or three-quarters in 1:12⅗, he would do just that. He didn't need to be worked in company. I have other horses that need that game-day situation in the morning, and I need to work them in company to keep them focused."

The things Howard observes in the barn are every bit as important as what a horse reveals to him in its training.

"I try to keep two steps ahead of my horses by being aware of season with an unblemished record in five starts. After that brilliant 2-year-old campaign, though, Howard encountered some turbulent times with him.

"Summer Squall was a precocious 2-year-old, and a very good 3-year-old," Howard said. "The only problem that kept Summer Squall from doing more was he was a bad bleeder. It was really a lesson learned. He was 5 for 5 as a 2-year-old, and never raced on Lasix as a 2-year-old. He came out of the Hopeful with a little hairline [fracture] of the cannon bone. He came back to me at Gulfstream and we were preparing him for his 3-year-old campaign. He was two or three works shy of his first race as a 3-year-old, and he came off the track gushing blood. I think that was the first time with a big horse that something so caught me by surprise. I said, 'Oh, man. Wait a minute here.'"

Primarily because of the bleeding problem, Campbell decided to pass on the Belmont Stakes after the colt's Preakness victory. Lasix was not legalized as a race-day medication in New York until 1995. In addition to the Preakness, Summer Squall won the Blue Grass, Jim Beam, and Pennsylvania Derby at 3. As a 4-year-old, he took the Fayette Handicap. He was retired to Lane's End with earnings of $1,844,282. Fertility problem; ended his stallion career in 2004, but not before he sired 199 Horse of the Year Charismatic, and Storm Song, the champic 2-year-old filly of 1994.

"Summer Squall was a remarkable horse for a small hors Howard said. "You talk about constitution, second to none. was a very easy horse to get ready; he was very willing. We him on Lasix, and basically did what you can with diffe medications to keep his lungs clear and cleansed, and so fc Because that is the thing about bleeding—bleeding lead more bleeding."

Howard said one of the luxuries of training for a bree

what is going on with them every day in the barn," he explained. "How their coats, appetite, and attitudes are will tell me if I should adjust or back off of them in their training. Those types of observations can send up a red flag and perhaps I won't do too much with them until I draw some blood to see what is going on."

Howard noted that his relationship with his vet is an important one, and it is imperative that the two share a rapport.

"A vet and a trainer really need to have a strong dialogue," he said. "I always defer to the vet in the end. On the flip side, a vet will defer to me when I might know better how a certain horse travels or what kind of habits a particular horse has. In the end, though, I never urge a vet to agree with me."

Farish cited the example of the way Howard managed Runup the Colors, another daughter of A.P. Indy and a half-sister to Mineshaft's dam, Prospectors Delite, as being indicative of his trainer's keen sense of treating each horse as an individual and recognizing and working with their strengths and weaknesses. The trainer opted to run her in the Delaware Oaks—against modest competition—before facing the accomplished filly Ajina in the 1997 Alabama.

"We took Runup the Colors to Delaware to prep her for the Alabama," Farish said. "She was pretty crooked in front, so Neil had to be very careful. He couldn't push too hard on her, but he got a race over a track that was heavier and kind of on the dull side. It got her fit to the point that she went on to win the Alabama.

"In a way, maybe having tougher competition on a surface like Delaware would have taken too much out of her," he added. "It was a kind of delicate situation. The track got her fitter, but she wasn't so hard-pressed. There were many situations like that with Neil. I think those types of decisions made it possible to pull off wins over the years."

The Alabama resulted in a stirring stretch battle from the furlong pole to the wire between Runup the Colors, who was seeking her fifth consecutive win, and Ajina, who owned wins in the Mother Goose and Coaching Club American Oaks. Runup the Colors gutted it out for a 1¼-length victory over Ajina, the 3-5 favorite, who subsequently earned the divisional title after defeating older fillies and mares in the Breeders' Cup Distaff at Hollywood Park.

Farish places a premium on developing fillies into stakes winners, because with any breeding operation the foundation begins with the broodmares. For Howard, winning the Alabama—one of the most coveted races in the country for owners and breeders of 3-year-old fillies—meant a job well done for his boss.

"When Runup the Colors won the Alabama, it was one of the most gratifying days of my career," Howard said. "She was all home cooking—100 percent owned and bred by Lane's End. For Mr. Farish, who puts so much into the breeding, to win a race like the Alabama, there is not much more you can say.

"Runup the Colors ran a helluva race in the Alabama. I was sitting behind the Farishes and I was watching him. I could see him. It wasn't so much that he was cheering, but I could see on his face how much it meant to him when they hit the wire. He is a historian by nature, and knows the history of this game. Those historical races, like the Alabama, are the backbone of the industry, and he holds that in such high regard. I wouldn't want to put words in his mouth, but I think he must think about that race at least once on a daily basis. That meant the world to him."

Farish and Howard nearly always take a conservative approach when placing their horses in stakes, and it is rare to see a Lane's End runner making a giant leap in class, or going off at double-digit odds while carrying Farish's green-and-yellow silks. Nevertheless, there are occasions when they will take a stab in a stakes if they believe their horse is worthy, and the field isn't overly laden with talent.

They ran Midway Road, who had no previous stakes wins, in the 2003 Preakness. At odds of 20-1, the second-longest price in the 10-horse field, Midway Road, named for the location of Lane's End Farm, finished second to Kentucky Derby winner Funny Cide. Although he was beaten 9¾ lengths, it was still an important placing for Midway Road's stallion resume.

Howard, Farish, and his partners Edward Hudson and Inwood Stables nearly pulled off a huge upset against another Kentucky Derby winner, Street Sense, in the 2007 Travers at Saratoga. They entered Grasshopper, who had no previous stakes experience and came into the $1 million Travers off a six-length victory in a second-level allowance race. Grasshopper, the fourth choice in the seven-horse field at 9-1, nearly stole the show after forging to the lead on the backstretch. What followed was one of those oh-so-familiar epic Saratoga stretch battles. Street Sense engaged Grasshopper at the top of the lane, and those two raced in tandem until Street Sense edged away in the final yards. Grasshopper, ridden by Albarado, finished second, beaten a half-length. He was 10¼ lengths clear of the third-place finisher, Helsinki.

"We knew we had a really good horse in Grasshopper," Farish said. "But because he had some minor illnesses along the way, we missed some training and subsequently some races. We got to Saratoga and the whole objective had not been to run in the Travers because he probably would not have been up to that. But we ran him in an allowance race and he ran extremely well.

"When you only have one major horse to beat in a stake, you

go for it. If you have three, you wait for another day. In the Travers, of course, the big challenge was Street Sense, and we took a shot and it almost worked. They were hooked up at the head of the stretch, and it was one of the most exciting stretch duels we have ever been involved in."

Little did Farish know when he uttered those words in April 2008 that four months later, another amazing stretch duel in the Travers was in store for him and Howard.

The 2008 Travers didn't have a standout like Street Sense, and the betting in the 12-horse field reflected that, with Pyro going off as the tepid 7-2 favorite. Howard, Farish, and co-owner Lora Jean Kilroy decided to take a shot with Mambo in Seattle. Although the colt had no graded stakes experience, he had scored a solid victory in an overnight stakes—his third consecutive win—on the Jim Dandy undercard 28 days earlier, and his final time was faster than that of Jim Dandy winner Macho Again.

Howard was very high on Mambo in Seattle, a son of Kingmambo whose second dam was Weekend Surprise. In the days leading up to the race, the trainer was uncharacteristically upbeat about the colt's chances, and radiated positive vibes to the media. Rarely does the conservative Howard talk up his horses, even if they are favorites on the morning line.

That Travers proved to be just about as dramatic a race as anyone saw during the 2008 Saratoga meet. The bulky field looked like bumper cars at the top of the stretch. Mambo in Seattle was hung out six-wide turning for home in the 10-furlong race after racing second-to-last down the backstretch. Colonel John wrested the lead from pacesetting Da' Tara, the Belmont Stakes winner, inside the eighth pole, but Mambo in Seattle was gobbling up ground, and for the final 100 yards, Colonel John and Mambo in Seattle's heads were bobbing like rocking-horses.

Albarado, aboard Mambo in Seattle, was so certain of the victory that he brandished his whip in jubilation—a premature move, because Mambo in Seattle lost by a nose in one of the closest photo finishes on record, according to Donald Morehouse, the longtime photo-finish operator for the New York Racing Association.

Forty-eight hours after the Travers, Howard had become more Zen about the loss than when the order of finish was first posted. His wife, Sue, however, was still feeling the pain of the tough beat.

"We've all been through the rodeo, but Sue took this one hard," Howard said. "I told her, 'You can't dwell because that does no good. I don't want to say he is a Mineshaft, but this horse will have his day. I can feel good we did the best that we could in that race.'"

Had Mambo in Seattle won the nose bob, it would have given a much-needed boost to the barn, which had suffered its worst year since Howard and Farish began their association. From 154 starters, there were only 11 winners. Mambo in Seattle, who won the ungraded Harry Walton Stakes at Saratoga, and Grasshopper, who won the Grade 3 Mineshaft Handicap at Fair Grounds, were the only stakes winners

"There are two sides to it," Howard said. "Any time you are a private trainer, especially for someone like the Farish family or the position Shug [McGaughey] is in with the Phipps family— there are only a handful of positions like that anyway—you are very fortunate. But there is no getting around the fact—even though I have some outside horses comprised of people that are affiliated with Mr. Farish—that if I have a year like 2008 you don't have the luxury, for lack of a better word, of spreading the bad news around. But that is part of it.

"It happens," he continued. "In an outfit like ours, you have a lot of homebreds and at some point you are going to be retiring horses—fillies that are going to the breeding shed and hopefully a couple of horses that go to stud. Everybody has ups and downs. We had some better horses retire, and in some years there are more injuries than other years. In some years, in January and February, you might think you have your best crop of 2-year-olds that you've ever had, and for the larger part, they don't pan out or are not what you think they were. On the other hand, early on you might think you don't have that much in the barn and you have your best bunch. That is what keeps you getting up in the morning. Mr. Farish goes to a lot of lengths to try to choose and earmark the right horses for the racing stable. So-so years are a part of the business. What is important is that you don't let it start changing your routine; that is the worst thing to do. You have to stick to that routine."

Howard is regarded as one of the good guys by the racing media because he is always available for interviews and never gets surly when the questions get tough. But he chooses his words carefully and there won't be any inflammatory statements or boastful words expressed by him. The one topic Howard has no reservations talking about, or expounding upon, is the man he has come to know so well.

"[Working for] Mr. Farish is like training for another trainer," Howard said. "He has done everything in this business. He's ridden every type of horse. He was one of the best polo players around. He understands exactly, and I understand, what the goals are. He understands what the obstacles are that can get in the way of achieving those goals. He is always clear as a bell about what he wants. Also, Mr. Farish likes to go back and forth on situations because it is the best way to arrive at the right decision. We always wind up making a decision that we are going to be able to live with. He taught me that. Every time that

NEIL HOWARD

VITAL STATISTICS

CATEGORY	STS.	W%	ROI
1stRaceTrn	2	0	0
180+Trn	7	0.14	0.91
61-180Trn	13	0.08	0.37
2nd45-180Lay	14	0.14	1.13
2nd180+Lay	3	0	0
1stStart	21	0.05	2.01
2ndMdn	17	0	0
MSWtoMCL	4	0	0
1stTurf	17	0.12	3.01
1stBlink	7	0	0
1stLasix	1	0	0
2YO	17	0	0
Dirt/Turf	11	0	0
Turf/Dirt	13	0	0
BlinkOn	8	0	0
BlinkOff	7	0	0
Sprint/Route	21	0.1	0.73
Route/Sprint	5	0	0
31-60Days	57	0.04	0.16
WonLast	15	0.2	1.81
Wet	19	0.05	0.32
Dirt	78	0.06	0.46
Turf	61	0.1	1.31
Sprints	32	0	0
Routes	130	0.09	0.94
MCL	7	0.14	0.46
MSW	84	0.04	0.69
Claim	5	0.2	1.36
ALW	36	0.14	1.23
STK	30	0.07	0.36
GSTK	19	0.05	0.25
DebutMCL	1	0	0
Debut>=1Mile	2	0.5	21.1
Synth	23	0.04	0.3
Turf/Synth	7	0	0
Synth/Turf	7	0.29	2.03

*January 1, 2008, through February 8, 2009, North American runners only

CAREER HIGHLIGHTS

BREEDERS' CUP

STARTS	1ST	2ND	3RD
5	0	0	0

TRIPLE CROWN

STARTS	1ST	2ND	3RD
5	1	2	0

WINNERS
Summer Squall: Preakness (1990)

ECLIPSE AWARDS
Mineshaft: Horse of the Year (2003);
Older Male (2003)

RECORDS/NOTABLE ACHIEVEMENTS
Was the leading trainer at Keeneland in the spring of 1994 (in a tie).

Was twice the leading trainer at Churchill Downs, in the fall of 1997 and 1998 (in a tie).

Saddled six consecutive winners during a six-day span in 1997 at Churchill Downs.

Won the 2000 Kentucky Oaks with Secret Status.

Reached 1,000 career wins on October 12, 2005, with Soul Search at Keeneland.

CAREER SUMMARY

STS	1ST	2ND	3RD	EARNINGS
5,273	1,077	853	748	$44,556,737

*Through February 8, 2009, North American runners only

he recommends something, he asks me if I am comfortable with it.

"I'm not going to sit here and tell you he is God. But the attributes I am talking about are [apparent], and not many people have them. He is a very intelligent man in a lot of areas of life. The proof has come out in what he has done with Lane's End."

Five

Allen Jerkens

On a dark-day afternoon at Belmont Park in the summer of 2008, Allen Jerkens was doing what he typically has done for the past 58 years when he isn't running a horse—holding the lead shank of a grazing Thoroughbred. Jerkens is always at his happiest spending some one-on-one time with his four-legged friends; he calls it "fooling with the horses." As Jerkens watched Dutchess of Rokeby, one of 36 runners in his stable, nibble grass, he reflected on the way racing's landscape has changed since he saddled his first winner, Populace, at Aqueduct on July 4, 1950. Jerkens, who was born April 21, 1929, fellow Hall of Famer Frank "Pancho" Martin, who is three years older, and Mike Hernandez, senior to them both, are the elder statesmen among New York trainers. Their contemporaries have either retired or died. Jerkens has been around so long that he has seen his day rate inflate from $16 per horse in 1962 to the $100 he charged in 2008.

"The owners here now are not the owners that were here when I first came around," Jerkens said, gazing around the quiet backstretch. "All these barns here were privately owned by the owners because they built them. I think the Phippses are still the only originals I can remember. I can't see anyone still around when I first came around. No more Calumet, Rokeby. I'm not even sure why this horse has Rokeby in her name. She doesn't have a thing to do with Rokeby."

The reminiscing from Jerkens whispers of a wistfulness for a bygone era. But while the trainer may be old-school by the standards of racing today, he can still comprehend the reasons that the grand stables, such as Calumet, Greentree, and Rokeby, have vanished and largely been replaced by syndicate groups.

"The tax situation for owners has changed," he said. "And the decendants of the owners, they are not into racing like their mothers and fathers were. They are into sports cars and boats. A lot of their wealth is handled by people who tell them it is not feasible to own horses. There are always people now coming into the game who pool their money, and they are having fun. That's the way it has to be now because it is so expensive."

Jerkens is familiar with training for syndicates. For a time he trained for Centennial Farms, whose winner's-circle photos nearly defy the capability of a camera lens with scores of partners jockeying for position to get a picture taken with "their" horse.

Jerkens is best known for his association with Jack Dreyfus, the proprietor of Hobeau Farm. Without a doubt, the relationship that Dreyfus and Jerkens forged in the early 1960s is one of the most enduring in racing. They hooked up when the late Pat Lynch, a former turf writer who was working for the New York Racing Association's publicity office, facilitated the introduction. Jerkens had been training for 12 years by then, and his stable was doing well enough that he wasn't entertaining thoughts of accepting a private training position.

"Pat Lynch said, 'I want you to meet a man who wants to have a trainer of his own.' I said, 'Oh, I don't want to do that,'" Jerkens recalled. "Pat said, 'Meet the guy anyway. He's got a farm; he is a fabulous guy, and he will put his money up and buy horses.' So I went to meet Jack in the city, Memorial Day, 1962. I didn't think we hit it off too good. I was a little cocky; I was the leading trainer in New York at the time. I was a wise guy. But I took the horses, and I have been with him ever since."

It was a smart play for Jerkens not to let his ego get in the way of accepting the opportunity of a lifetime. For nearly 20 years, he worked solely for Dreyfus, who was the chairman of the New York Racing Association in 1969 and 1975. Dreyfus, the founder of the Dreyfus Fund, which popularized mutual funds by becoming the first investment house to launch ad campaigns in the 1950s, cut back on his racing stock in 1980 and told Jerkens he could accept other clients. In 2008, Jerkens trained about 10 homebreds for Dreyfus, and fondly recalled the bustling days when Hobeau was at its prime.

"[Dreyfus] had a couple of fast fillies, including Beauful and Red Bell," Jerkens said. "I loved fast fillies. I had the idea I could make them go the distance, and Red Bell and Beauful both did that. In fact, we lost Beauful in a claimer, and we bought her back because Jack liked her, and she won the 1964 Bed o' Roses. He lost her for $16,000 and bought her back for $40,000. One thing about Jack, he was bold."

Before Dreyfus came along and paid Jerkens a salary and covered all the stable's expenses, Jerkens had a prosperous relationship with owner Eddie Seinfeld, who would frequently claim horses. One of their sharper moves was claiming Admiral Vee for $7,500 and then putting him through a campaign that yielded more than $200,000 and six stakes wins, including the 1958 Saratoga Handicap.

"Mr. Seinfeld was good to work for because we had a good rapport," Jerkens said. "At that time, we claimed horses and he was patient with me. He never played the red-board on you; he was awfully nice that way. I was young when I started training for Mr. Seinfeld, and he would never say 'I told you so.' In those days, when I saw something I didn't like about a horse, I would put him in a claiming race. He would say, 'How come all of a sudden you want to put him in a claiming race? How do you blow so hot and cold?' That was his favorite thing to say."

It was through his connection with Dreyfus, however, that Jerkens became a racing legend. Many of their horses found their way into the history books, starting with Beau Purple, who defeated five-time Horse of the Year Kelso on three occasions (1962 Suburban, 1962 Man o' War, and 1963 Widener). In 1973, both Onion and Prove Out upset Secretariat, the first Triple Crown winner since Citation in 1948. Jerkens and Dreyfus also stunned the brilliant Buckpasser with Handsome Boy, who beat the champion in his penultimate career start, the 1967 Brooklyn Handicap. Handsome Boy left Buckpasser, the runner-up, eight lengths in his wake in the 1¼-mile Brooklyn, while in receipt of 20 pounds from the Ogden Phipps home-bred.

Jerkens earned the nickname of Giant Killer for those successes and other upsets he has pulled off during his career. He dislikes the label, but as he mellows with age—or maybe he is just weary of fighting it—he has reluctantly accepted the moniker. He gladly accepts being called Chief, which a pony boy in his employ started calling him in the 1960s. A new generation of workers calls him Boss Man around the barn. No one ever addresses him by his given name, Harry.

"Well, the way I look at it, when your horse doesn't win, I'm always thinking people are making fun of you for being called Giant Killer. There are so many people who once in a while have horses that beat one of the champions and they don't call them that. It's not fair, really. Well, anyway, I'll take it. What the hell.

"I'll never forget some girl from television who came by the barn when I didn't think we had a chance the next day. We were in the [2001] Ballerina with Shine Again. And she said, 'I want to hear you say Giant Killer.' And I said, 'I will not.' She said, 'C'mon, just say it for me . . . Giant Killer.' So I said, 'Giant Killer.' She said, 'That's good; that's a wrap.' Then she said, 'You're the Budweiser Longshot,' and sure enough, Shine Again won the next day."

Shine Again, who went off at 21-1, was owned by the late Allaire DuPont's Bohemia Stable. (DuPont had owned Kelso, but must have forgiven Jerkens for beating her grand gelding three times in the 1960s, since she later gave him horses to train.) Shine Again also won the Ballerina in 2002, but at a more modest 3-1.

Jerkens doesn't pretend that he is predicting an upset when he enters horses to run against powerhouses. The school of thought runs more along the lines of taking a shot, particularly when the field might only feature one standout. But perhaps one of the reasons that Onion's victory over Secretariat in the 1973 Whitney Handicap at Saratoga is one of Jerkens's most satisfying moments in the business is because he sensed the colt might have been vulnerable after his Triple Crown campaign, despite Secretariat's easy victory over a small field in the Arlington Invitational 21 days after his record-shattering Belmont romp.

Like any good trainer, Jerkens scopes out his competition, and he was keeping a keen eye on Secretariat that summer at Saratoga as Lucien Laurin prepared the Meadow Stable champion for the Whitney.

"Funny part was I thought Secretariat might have had enough," Jerkens said. "He had been through the Triple Crown and then he went to Chicago. For some reason he worked a mile in 34 for the Whitney, and I think Laurin was livid about that. Something happened there.

"Three days before the Whitney, he went a half in 48 [⅕] and I was there. Everyone said [the rider] was trying to make him go as slow as he could, but I saw his arms moving. You know Gargantua couldn't have worked him a half in 48 when he was really right. I'm not saying I thought I could beat him or anything. I was going into a stakes where a big horse would scare others out, and there was a chance to be second or third."

Although Onion had never won a stakes race, Jerkens knew he was in sharp form, since the 4-year-old gelding had broken Saratoga's track record for 6½ furlongs just four days earlier. The Whitney drew a field of only five, and Secretariat was the overwhelming favorite of the record crowd of 30,119, going off at 1-10 under regular rider Ron Turcotte. Second choice Onion, with Jacinto Vasquez in the irons and carrying equal weight of 119 pounds with Secretariat, led throughout and defeated the Triple Crown winner by one length, returning $13.20. In the aftermath of the race, it was widely reported that Secretariat had been harboring a virus at the time.

Secretariat looked like his old self in his next start, the Marlboro Cup Invitational Handicap at Belmont on September 15, defeating a field that included Onion as well as champions Cougar II, Key to the Mint, and Riva Ridge—his stablemate— and setting a world record for 1⅛ miles. His next scheduled race was supposed to be the Man o' War in October, his grass debut,

but when the track came up sloppy for the September 29 Woodward, Laurin and owner Penny Tweedy scratched Riva Ridge, whose off-track form was dismal, and ran Secretariat off just two leisurely turf workouts.

As in the Whitney, only four other horses showed up, and once again Jerkens was ready to pounce—albeit with a seemingly unlikely challenger. About a week after defeating Secretariat at Saratoga with Onion, Jerkens and Dreyfus privately bought 4-year-old Prove Out, a horse with problematic ankles, from Bob Kleberg of the famous King Ranch and his trainer, Buddy Hirsch.

"I just couldn't do anything right with this colt, and I told Mr. Kleberg we should get rid of him," Hirsch told *Sports Illustrated*'s Whitney Tower in October 1973. "I got a man to pay $65,000, but I told the boss, 'This is a dangerous man to sell a horse to; he's apt to jump up and make anyone look bad.'"

Between the time of the purchase and the Woodward, Prove Out made four starts for Jerkens, and won two of them, including an upset over Forego on August 24, setting a Saratoga track record of 1:21 for seven furlongs in an allowance race. He had problems with lugging in, however, and after he hit the rail in the Chesapeake Handicap at Bowie, Jerkens switched to Jorge Velasquez, the leading stakes-winning rider in New York at the time, and removed Prove Out's blinkers.

"In a long race, horses find it more difficult to settle down when they have blinkers on," Jerkens told Tower.

Prove Out was conceding seven pounds to Secretariat and stretching out from 1$\frac{1}{16}$ miles to a mile and a half, but with the blinkers off, he relaxed for Velasquez and set a slow pace, getting the first half-mile in 50 seconds flat. Secretariat took the lead with a rush on the backstretch, opening up by two lengths, but with a quarter of a mile to run Prove Out was gaining on the inside. Secretariat fought back briefly, but Prove Out ran by him and pulled off a 4½-length upset at 16-1, stunning nearly everyone—including his trainer.

"I still can't believe it. It doesn't seem real," said Jerkens in *Sports Illustrated*.

It was the last race Secretariat would lose. Nine days later, he won the Man o' War by five lengths, setting yet another world record, but the pair of upsets over the two-time Horse of the Year earned Jerkens the Eclipse Award as top trainer of 1973. Two years later, he entered the Hall of Fame at the age of 45, becoming the youngest trainer at the time to receive that honor.

Jerkens cites Dreyfus as being one of the two most influential people in his life. The other was his father, Joseph, who operated a riding academy on Long Island's South Shore. In addition to the show horses and pleasure horses he kept in his barn, the elder Jerkens—an Austrian cavalry captain before emigrating to the United States—also nursed lay-up horses off the racetrack. A year after Allen Jerkens received his trainer's license, his father died.

"We had horses that broke down and we would take them in the water on Great South Bay," Jerkens said. "A lot of them came back to race. Then I got to thinking racehorses all the time. I said to my father when I was 16 that I wanted to go to the track, and he said, 'Why do you want to do that?' I began galloping horses when school was out. Then I just didn't go back to school. My mother died when I was 15. I asked my father, 'Tell me something I can find out about training horses in school.' As it turns out, most people who have an education do better than me because they know how to run a business. I'm terrible at that part, but it has never bothered me either."

It's true that visitors to Jerkens's barn are not going to find him behind a desk in the office, shooting off e-mails to his owners about the progress of their runners. In a nod to modern technology, Jerkens does carry a cell phone, and has his own web site, but as his wife, Elisabeth, points out, the cell phone's mailbox becomes jammed with messages, and her husband is at a loss to find the erase button that would allow new callers to get in touch.

Something else Jerkens is not so great at is being a good patient. In December 2000, he was stricken with acute pancreatitis and spent a month in the intensive-care unit of a Florida hospital. By the second week of February 2001, Jerkens was making visits to the barn, despite doctors' orders to the contrary. In the spring of that year, he was back to full speed.

Not surprisingly, Jerkens only had one thing on his mind during his convalescence: his horses.

"I kept wondering what was going on out there," he said. "You don't realize how lucky you are when you are in a slump; it's so much better than being in the hospital. The thing that worried me the most when I was in there was when they tried to get me up to walk; I felt like I was paralyzed, like I would never be able to move again. I was weak; by God it was scary."

He said he wasn't even able to stay in touch with goings-on at his stable by phone for the first two weeks because he was so knocked out from medications that he couldn't remember anything.

"I had the funniest dreams of where I was," he said. "I dreamt I was at the old Hialeah track, and it was still running. I thought I had landed in New York on a plane with my horses. I thought I was staying in the third floor of the clubhouse at Gulfstream. I don't know why I had a hospital room there."

As he regained some strength, however, hospital workers surely suffered some anxious moments when Jerkens, who is well over six feet tall and is solidly built, had to be restrained from getting out of his bed so that he could get back to his horses.

In October 2008, Jerkens found himself back in the hospital, this time on Long Island, undergoing heart surgery to repair two valves and implant a pacemaker. In true Jerkens fashion, the afternoon he was released from the rehabilitation center that he had entered after his hospital stay, he immediately went to Belmont Park to see his horses. Jerkens sat on a bench outside the barn as each of his horses was paraded before him for his inspection.

By January 2009, Jerkens, who winters in Florida, was back at his Gulfstream Park base on a daily basis. Early one morning during the meet, he sat in a golf cart outside his barn, rattling off instructions to exercise riders heading to the track. As each horse walked by, Jerkens recited its full pedigree for his visitors, and his eyes lit up at the sight of a handsome chestnut colt he thought had a promising future.

"Heck, you never know about these horses, but you keep hoping," Jerkens said, his eyes never leaving his trainees as they circled the shed row.

Although Jerkens is not a meek person, he is reserved with strangers, and can come across as very quiet by nature and uncomfortable in front of a crowd. When he was honored by the National Turf Writers Association in 2001, he was on and off the stage in less than 30 seconds with a brief "Hello, thank you, good-bye." That doesn't mean he doesn't have a quick temper, although he says it has abated somewhat as he has gotten older. Usually, jockeys are at the receiving end of his tantrums, and many fellow trainers—along with owners, other jockeys, valets, grooms, and members of the press—have witnessed the sight of a red-faced Jerkens waving his trademark straw hat wildly in the air while bellowing at a rider in the Belmont tunnel after a losing effort.

"I ain't proud of that," he said. "One thing about that, I don't take them off and never say anything to the press about them. I never knocked a jock in the press ever. Even one time in New England when I went there for the 1967 Massachusetts Handicap and the riders ran them into the ground.

"It was Handsome Boy and Beau Legs. Willie Mayorga and Leroy Moyers were the riders," he recalled. Mayorga was riding Beau Legs and Moyers was aboard Handsome Boy; both horses were trained by Jerkens.

"It was Willie's fault; he rode Beau Legs and kept after Handsome Boy. He shoved him down in the deep going. It was unbelievable. It was like they were doing it on purpose. The press called the next day and asked if I would ride those jockeys again. I said, 'I guess I probably will.' And I did.

"A lot of times you get hot at the jockey. That's why it doesn't pay to go near them until at least the next day. Now I can't get down [to the track] after the race anyway, because I can't walk that fast."

But there have also been many acts of kindness from Jerkens toward riders, and his staff. He can cuss out a hotwalker for yanking on the shank too hard, but is reaching in his pocket the next moment to give his employee money for a hot breakfast.

Hall of Fame rider Angel Cordero Jr. recalls when he was trying to snag yet another riding title in New York, he implored Jerkens to give him live mounts to get the job done, and the trainer would say, "What? I'm giving out charity rides now?" But Jerkens always came through when he could for Cordero, who said that under the trainer's gruff exterior is a teddy bear of a man.

"The thing is that Allen will yell after a race, but the next morning it's over and done with," said Cordero, who is now a jockey's agent for one of the country's leading riders, John

Velazquez. "I never talked back to him. I remember someone asking me, 'How can you stand it?' I told them, 'He's the Chief, and I respect him.'"

Cordero said a testament to Jerkens's popularity among riders is that when the trainer wins a race, everyone is cheering for him in the jockeys' room.

"There is not one other trainer they would do that for," Cordero said.

Something that might be perplexing to Jerkens's owners, as well as horseplayers, is his penchant for using inexperienced riders—not just in claiming and allowance races, but also in stakes. The names Ray Ganpath, Shannon Uske, and Noel Wynter will probably not be rolling off the tongues of racing historians in years to come, but they have all ridden Jerkens-trained stakes winners. When the 30-year-old Ganpath won the Grade 1 Frizette for Jerkens aboard Society Selection in 2003, reporters on deadline were scrambling to get biographical information on the unknown from Trinidad who galloped horses for Jerkens in the mornings.

Wynter was aboard the speedy Put It Back when he won the 2001 Riva Ridge Stakes. Uske was 17 when she rode her first winner, the Jerkens-trained Lilah, in an optional claimer at Calder in 2003. Jerkens even used Uske aboard Lilah in a couple of New York graded stakes that yielded paychecks, if not victories.

Lilah did win a stakes in 2005 under another Jerkens protégé; he spotted the potential in the unseasoned Rajiv Maragh, a five-pound apprentice, and they teamed to win the 2005 Hurricane Bertie, a Grade 3 at Gulfstream Park. Maragh has since become a top rider in New York.

Jerkens said there is a method behind what many perceive as . . . well, if not madness, then at least quirkiness.

"Say you have a horse, and based on form, the jockey thinks you must be nuts for running them," he said. "If you put one of the leading riders on, he is not going to have a confident attitude. Whereas if you have a guy [who is] just getting started and wants to show he is good, he will give a horse a better ride than someone who is famous. I don't know; I might be overdoing that in my own mind."

Another of Jerkens's trademarks is working a horse swiftly—a blowout of three furlongs or less—a day or two before a race, or opting for a mile breeze four or five days before a race, rather than the common four-, five-, or six-furlong moves employed by most trainers. The concept of the short blowout is something he picked up during his days of playing polo, when the ponies would be given their heads and "go as fast as they could go" for an eighth of a mile before a match would begin. Jerkens believes that rather than taking too much zip out of a horse, a sharp work usually picks up his head and puts him on his toes. He said it doesn't work for every horse, and he picks his spots when deciding if a runner will benefit from that practice.

There have been instances in which Jerkens didn't plan on a snappy work in the days before a race, but rider error dictated otherwise. A case in point was Beau Purple, who beat Kelso and 1962 Kentucky Derby and Preakness winner Carry Back in that year's Suburban.

"Beau Purple worked a mile in 1:37 two days before he beat Kelso and Carry Back," Jerkens said. "I planned on him working a mile in 1:42, and I was up in the stands and was waving to the exercise rider. He was a good little guy, George Wallace. Later he said, 'I didn't see you, I didn't see you.' I said, 'George, you messed it up now. We've blown the race.' He said, 'It was just what he needed.' Guess he was right. Beau Purple was a little fat horse. You could see if you didn't do anything with him for a week or so, he would belly right down.

"Probably the ideal thing is if you work the horse three or four days before the race and they work good," he added. "Then you're safe because you don't have to worry about someone going too fast the day before the race. Sometimes if you do that and they go [three-eighths] in 33 and change, you do take too much zip out of them."

Jerkens is a big believer in sticking to a routine with his horses. That paid off with Sky Beauty, the only Eclipse Award winner he has trained, and the work he did with her is still one of his greatest sources of satisfaction. As a 3-year-old in 1993, the daughter of 1988 Alabama winner Maplejinsky won the Acorn, Mother Goose, and Coaching Club American Oaks at Belmont, a prestigious trio known as the New York Filly Triple Crown until the late 1980s, when it was renamed the Triple Tiara. Coming up to the Alabama at Saratoga, however, Sky Beauty started acting finicky at the feed tub, and Jerkens was second-guessing himself. But in the end, he didn't allow his trepidation to alter his training schedule with the filly, who was owned by Georgia Hofmann.

"That was one of my most nervous times in my lifetime, getting ready for the Alabama; she had stopped eating," Jerkens recalled. "I said to Mrs. Hofmann maybe we shouldn't run. She said, 'Oh, we have to run. We have planned so much for this. Her mother won it.' But I said, 'Yeah, it doesn't work that way, Mrs. Hofmann.' I used to give Sky Beauty a strong work five or six days before her races. I was thinking I shouldn't do it. But I never won a big race in my life when I hedged. I gave her a good work; she went a mile in 1:39 or 1:38. She started to eat. Sometimes horses are better when you put the pressure on them."

Sky Beauty won the Alabama by 1½ lengths and added yet

another victory back at Belmont Park in the Rare Perfume. In most years, winning five graded stakes in a row would have been good enough for an Eclipse Award, but Sky Beauty fumbled when it counted the most for voters by finishing fifth in the Breeders' Cup Distaff at Santa Anita. The Distaff winner, Hollywood Wildcat, earned the 3-year-old championship for beating older fillies and mares, but Sky Beauty would win her own title the following year. She returned for a brilliant 4-year-old campaign that included Grade 1 wins in the Shuvee, Hempstead, Go for Wand, and Ruffian.

The year before Sky Beauty took the Alabama, Jerkens won the race with November Snow, who completed a difficult Saratoga stakes double with that victory. November Snow became only the 12th filly to win the seven-furlong Test Stakes and the 10-furlong Alabama, which were run just two weeks apart. To prepare a horse to successfully tackle an additional three furlongs, plus another turn, in a Grade 1 race, is not an easy feat, but Jerkens did it twice, with November Snow and Society Selection.

The Alabama was first run in 1872, while the Test debuted in 1922, and since then the number of fillies who have won both races has been limited to a baker's dozen, including champions Vagrancy, Stefanita, Desert Vixen, and Go for Wand. Society Selection became number 13 by defeating a field that included future champion Ashado in 2004, when there were three weeks between the two races.

"Society Selection was one of my favorite horses," Jerkens said. "Winning the Test and the Alabama the same year was a big thrill. Everything had to go right. Shannon [Uske] worked Society Selection a mile the Monday before the Alabama and did it perfectly, too. November Snow, I didn't know what to do with her, so I just gave her a couple of really strong and fast gallops.

"It is almost impossible to win [races] close together because the thinking now is not to run back quick. But they did it a lot, years ago."

Jerkens has little patience for today's practice of micromanaging a horse's number of starts in order to have him at his prime for the year-end goal of the Breeders' Cup.

"I had a good filly, Blessing Angelica, who ran five times in six weeks, and won the Diana and Delaware Handicaps the same year," Jerkens said. "Now when trainers are asked 'When are you going to run him back?' they say, 'I might run him back once at Saratoga and then in another race and then the Breeders' Cup.'

"Sometimes so many things happen to the horse anyway to prevent you from running. You know, to hear people talk, they don't think anything can happen in the meantime. A horse can get loose on the track. It rains the day you want to work them. They get a quarter crack at the wrong time.

"If a horse is doing well, looks well, is sound, and there is a race to run them in, there is no reason not to, I think," he continued. "If he loses weight or is sore, then you don't run him. Trainers like Ben Jones and Max Hirsch ran them every time they were doing well and there was a race for them. You can put something in the freezer and take it out when you want to eat it, but that doesn't work with horses.

"The fact that all the owners think everyone should do the same thing, like that much time in between races, is one of the things I don't like about the game now. Owners have the right to a say because they are putting up their money. But you still have to strike a happy medium. The trainers are the ones with the horses and then an owner will say you shouldn't run. The horse is doing good and the race is right there, staring at you in the condition book. There are different plays in the game that you can only make if you are on the scene.

"When I do things my way and they don't work, [owners] say it's my fault. That's what happens in sports. Turn on a sports show and the owner is telling the manager what to do with a baseball team. It is more the trend in every sport now. You live with it if you love the game enough."

It is probably safe to assume that the "bounce" theory, which presumes that horses who earn big speed figures are thus considered vulnerable in their next starts, was not a concept that Ben Jones and Max Hirsch, two of the greatest trainers of the 20th century, would have bought. Not surprisingly, Jerkens pooh-poohs what he considers to be an overused excuse.

"Another thing today is that everything bounces," Jerkens said. "You can run a maiden and win and beat nobody, and then you run him a month later, and then he doesn't win and everyone says he bounces. That is a lot of baloney. If a horse bounces it's because he extends himself too much, had a hard ride. That is a reason to bounce."

"Baloney" was also a word Jerkens used to describe the recent controversy over using steroids in Thoroughbreds, a topic that drew intense scrutiny from federal regulators in the summer of 2008. Jerkens thought the issue was much ado about nothing.

"They have been giving steroids to horses for 50 years," he said. "I've given steroids to my horses when my vet and I think a horse is getting a little thin. We get a horse going good, and I haven't seen [giving] steroids has done harm. How come you can drink milk from a cow that was given steroids, and it's okay for you? If they decide to cut out steroids for horses that's okay, too."

While Jerkens scoffs at modern ideas such as the bounce theory and the practice of spacing horses' races with surgical precision, some of his beliefs might seem curious to younger generations of trainers. For instance, he claims that there is a connection between the full moon and the behavior of fillies. Teammate, a Joe Allen-owned homebred who won the 2007 Shuvee Handicap at Belmont Park and was third in that year's Spinster at Keeneland before finishing 11th in the Breeders' Cup Distaff at Monmouth Park, would get goofy when the moon was at its fullest.

"Teammate, she would get to jumping," Jerkens said. "The [night] watchman would call and say, 'This filly is going crazy. What do you want me to do with her?' I would come out and put her in the outdoor pen and fool around with her. She would do that every once in a while. I always said if they get their female cycle, the same time it is a full moon, and maybe the same time they [breeze]—all together—sometimes they can't handle it. I could be wrong about that, but I think it has something to do with it."

Another problem that he often encounters with fillies is tie-up syndrome (also known as exertional rhabdomyolysis), which can afflict both male and female horses, but is particularly prevalent in the latter. Horses tie up when an excess of lactic acid builds in the body, causing spasms in the muscles that power horses' hind legs. A horse becomes reluctant to move forward when this occurs.

Jerkens recalled one filly in particular, a stakes winner named Miss Shop, who chronically tied up.

"Miss Shop was pretty difficult to train because she had the tie-up syndrome," Jerkens said. "You know, the tie-up syndrome horses are the toughest horses to train because if you don't do something with them every day, they are more liable to tie up. If you give them a rest, they will tie up more. You don't give them a rest and then they get overtrained.

"It is so hard to strike the right medium with them," he added.

"Sometimes they tie up when they get their female cycle; and sometimes because it's a full moon and sometimes it happens when the track is muddy. Any little thing that sets them off can cause it.

"Another horse I had, Summer Secretary, was like that, too. She tied up the morning she won the [1991] Beaugay, and if I hadn't been around a long time, I might have scratched. It used to be that if I had a horse that would tie up anytime near a race, I would scratch them. But there are a lot of horses that tie up close to a race, and will run well."

After nearly six decades of dealing with the idiosyncrasies of Thoroughbreds, Jerkens has become philosophical about his profession.

"One thing about training horses, you can do it the opposite way and still win, or do everything right and still lose. It's the same thing with shipping in a week ahead of time for a race. Someone comes in six hours before the race on a 200-mile trip and they still beat you. It's a mysterious thing training horses. It is hard to do the right thing."

Shipping isn't something Jerkens does often, and in fact, a perusal of his career stakes wins doesn't yield many races won outside New York and Florida. Jerkens said his reluctance to ship has nothing to do with a travel phobia.

"We generally have the same races in New York and Florida that you would find elsewhere," he said. "We didn't used to have those overnight stakes we do now in New York, so we had to ship around to get horses black type. I never could see shipping just to ship."

Jerkens has sired two trainers, Jimmy and Steve, who both operate stables in New York. A third son, Allen, is a sportscaster in Oklahoma. Jimmy's twin, Julie, is a schoolteacher in Florida.

Jimmy and his father are occasional rivals in major stakes, and a particularly compelling father-son battle took place in the 2007 Metropolitan Handicap. Jimmy trained Corinthian, the winner; Allen trained the runner-up, Political Force. The "Met Mile" set the stage for a rematch in the Suburban Handicap. Corinthian was favored, but this time Dad posted a mild upset with the Joe Allen-owned Political Force.

Allen said, "Sure, I'm happy when Jimmy wins, but it's also okay to beat him, too."

Corinthian later won the inaugural running of the 2007 Breeders' Cup Dirt Mile at Monmouth Park, which probably added some delayed gratification to having beaten him. In addition, the victory by Political Force may have been that much more satisfying since Corinthian was owned by Centennial Farms, who fired Allen in the early 1990s and transferred seven horses to the barn of the late Scotty Schulhofer. Jerkens said the trainer change stung. One of the runners taken from Jerkens was Rubiano, who won the 1992 Eclipse Award as top sprinter for Schulhofer and Centennial.

"I felt awful bad when Centennial fired me," Jerkens said. "I thought I was doing okay. We tried Rubiano on the turf. That was the day before I got fired. He didn't run good on the grass. I don't think [Jerry] Bailey even rode him good, but that is beside the point. I guess it wasn't meant to be."

Jerkens said one of the things he has learned about training is not to pull out a bag of tricks when his stable is going through a slump. Still, he admits it is difficult to stick with the status quo when horses aren't firing. Another lesson learned is not to get too comfortable with success.

"[Dreyfus] is the one that warned me about that," Jerkens said. "He told me when you change from what made you successful in the first place, you are liable to keep in a slump. But

ALLEN JERKENS

VITAL STATISTICS

CATEGORY	STS.	W%	ROI
1stNAStart	3	0	0
1stRaceTrn	13	0.15	1.6
180+Trn	16	0.06	0.25
61-180Trn	22	0.14	0.88
2nd45-180Lay	28	0.18	2.28
2nd180+Lay	15	0.2	1.99
1-7Last	11	0.09	0.57
1stStart	31	0.06	0.62
2ndMdn	27	0.07	0.63
MSWtoMCL	11	0.27	3.05
1stTurf	20	0.1	1.43
1stBlink	12	0	0
1stLasix	22	0.05	0.26
2YO	30	0.03	0.19
Dirt/Turf	39	0.1	1.07
Turf/Dirt	34	0.18	2.45
BlinkOn	14	0	0
BlinkOff	2	0.5	2.4
Sprint/Route	48	0.04	0.25
Route/Sprint	44	0.14	1.39
Sprint2/Route	7	0	0
31-60Days	57	0.18	1.74
WonLast	35	0.11	1.16
Wet	46	0.17	1.73
Dirt	222	0.12	1.16
Turf	105	0.09	1
Sprints	205	0.13	1.21
Routes	123	0.07	0.93
MCL	56	0.12	1.5
MSW	80	0.1	0.9
Claim	53	0.11	1.11
ALW	95	0.12	1.15
STK	37	0.11	1.05
GSTK	24	0.08	1.22
DebutMCL	10	0	0
Debut>=1Mile	3	0	0
Synth	1	0	0

*January 1, 2008, through February 8, 2009, North American runners only

CAREER HIGHLIGHTS

BREEDERS' CUP

STARTS	1ST	2ND	3RD
11	0	1	0

TRIPLE CROWN

STARTS	1ST	2ND	3RD
6	0	0	0

ECLIPSE AWARDS
Leading Trainer (1973)
Sky Beauty: Older Filly or Mare (1994)

RECORDS/NOTABLE ACHIEVEMENTS
Inducted into racing Hall of Fame (1975) at age 45; at that time, he was the youngest trainer to receive that honor.

Was the leading trainer in New York in 1957, 1962, 1966, and 1969.

Won three Grade 1 races and $1,939,120 in 1993 with Devil His Due, who won the overall title in the final year of the American Championship Racing Series.

Tied with Shug McGaughey for most NYRA stakes victories in 1993 with 14.

Through 2008, he ranked 11th in all-time wins (3,758) and 12th in purse money earned ($98,863,277).

CAREER SUMMARY

STS	1ST	2ND	3RD	EARNINGS
20,172	3,762	2,764	2,433	$98,994,920

*Through February 8, 2009, North American runners only

if you are feeding vitamins and making mash, and picking [dandelion] greens for feed, and still not winning, you think, 'What good is all this stuff?' There will always be someone else who looks like he is half-trying and winning a lot. There always seems to be someone like that in the game. You are always thinking and worrying. When you have a public stable there is always some owner you can't do good for. It was different years ago when whatever races I won, they were for Jack.

"That is another thing about training, every once in a while, as you go along, you might get complacent. That is one thing you can't do in this game. You can't get one single bit complacent. It will come back and haunt you every time.

"But I will tell you this, as much as you think the business has changed, it really hasn't changed. The good horses win. It's still a horse game, no matter what they say."

Six

Carl Nafzger

Bull riding is often referred to as the most dangerous eight seconds in sports. The Kentucky Derby is billed as the most exciting two minutes in sports. As a former rodeo champion and two-time winner of the Kentucky Derby, Hall of Fame trainer Carl Nafzger can tell you firsthand about both experiences.

On August 4, 2008, the morning after the induction ceremony at the National Museum of Racing in Saratoga Springs, New York, Nafzger and his wife, Wanda, were relaxing on the backstretch of Saratoga Race Course. Watching the horses trained by his former assistant, Ian Wilkes, return to the barn after their exercise, the 66-year-old trainer reflected on what had occurred less than 24 hours earlier. As he had done at the induction, Nafzger paid homage to the horse.

"The horse has taken us from Texas, all the way to the Hall," he said. "Believe me: The horses have taken us every step of the way. You can't go any higher than being inducted into the Thoroughbred Racing Hall of Fame as a trainer. It's the highest honor that the industry can give you."

The Hall of Fame journey began for Nafzger, who was the son of a rancher and farmer in Olton, Texas, 40 years earlier when he took out his trainer's license. That same year he married Wanda, whom he had met during his days as a professional bull rider. In fact, another Hall of Fame called on Nafzger in 2008; he was also recognized for his prowess in the rodeo ring (he ranked third in the world in 1963) with an induction into the Texas Rodeo Hall of Fame.

Two and a half years earlier, Nafzger, who had trained one Kentucky Derby winner and two Eclipse Award winners, decided to go into semi-retirement, turning the bulk of the horses in his care over to Wilkes. In 2008, he was still training 10 horses in total for two of his longtime clients, James Tafel and Bentley Smith. It was a good thing that he didn't fully retire, because in 2007, Tafel provided the trainer with his second Derby winner, Street Sense.

After cutting back on the number of horses in his barn, Nafzger refocused his attention on a side of the business that had always appealed to him. In 1996, Carl and Wanda launched Traits LLC, which continues to function as a business enterprise for people wishing to become owners of racehorses. The name Traits is a nod to the 1994 book written by Nafzger, *Traits of a Winner*, which chronicles his formula for developing racehorses. The Nafzgers cultivate the owners and scout racing prospects. Wilkes, a native of Australia who began galloping horses in the late 1980s for Nafzger, is the trainer for Traits LLC. Wilkes quipped, "I'm the only trainer with a Hall of Fame trainer for an assistant."

Nafzger said he doesn't miss the 24/7 demands of training

racehorses because the new direction he and Wanda have taken is just as rewarding.

"We like to take people and put them in the business so they can enjoy it, and nobody can enjoy this business if they do it in a financial bind," Nafzger said. "So we try to take people and explain to them what they need to do to get out of that financial bind, where the kids' college money is going down the drain on a horse. We manage the horses, develop the horses, and put a program together that is not any different than any other business program that has to perform as a speculative investment model. Racing can be a good financial speculative investment. So many people don't think this business is a good investment. It can be a great speculative investment, and an enjoyable investment."

It is in Nafzger's nature to be realistic, and his pragmatism kicked in when he came to the conclusion that his body could sustain the rigors of riding bulls for only so long. Their sole mission was to launch him airborne as quickly as possible, and during his 10-year career in the ring, one such incident resulted in a steel rod being inserted in one of Nafzger's legs to repair a fracture.

"I didn't just throw my rope down one day and walk off and never get on another bull," he said. "I gradually worked my way down, trying to see if I wanted to stay in rodeo. Wanda was teaching school, and I was riding bulls. But I was working at other things. I went to Cal Poly and took a shoeing class. You shoe horses, build your own shoes, and study the physiology of the horse. I was about 26 then. I knew it was time to go on to something else other than bull riding. Any athlete has a limited career. I said at the time that the next career that I get into has to be an asset when I get older, instead of a detriment. That's where training came in, because you never quit learning, and always keep building."

Nafzger took out his trainer's license in 1968, but he got off to a discouraging start. In the spring of that year, the Nafzgers, who were newlyweds, had one horse, largely because they were only allotted one stall at Ruidoso Downs in New Mexico. By August, that one horse, who hadn't won a race, was returned to his owner because the Nafzgers were feeling the pinch financially. Nafzger continued to spend some time in the rodeo ring and also shod horses while Wanda worked as a special-education teacher. In 1970, they made the decision to pool their resources with Nafzger's father and his two brothers, Don and J. P., and buy two yearlings at Keeneland. The family left Texas in a two-horse trailer and headed for Lexington, Kentucky, with $8,000. They spent all but $500.

"We started out in the horse business to build a band of 10 broodmares because we figured 10 mares would be worth 100 cows," Nafzger said. "If we did a good job, worked hard, took good care of our babies, raised good colts, we had an intrinsic value on whatever we could do. That was a very strong drawing point for Wanda and me. There are two things that are really neat about horses, and I am talking about financially. You can appreciate their value, if you handle them right. A horse always has an intrinsic value. Never can there be a set price on a horse. Those two things fascinate us."

Business picked up in the 1970s when Nafzger received some horses from a ranch owner in Wyoming. Nafzger won his first stakes race—the La Fiesta Derby—with Speedy Karen at Santa Fe Downs in New Mexico in 1971. When things continued to go well, the Nafzgers, who have always been motivated by setting goals, started to look beyond the Southwest, and began racing horses in the Midwest and on the East Coast.

Nafzger's career was ignited when he began an association with John Nerud, the retired Hall of Fame trainer who worked for the legendary Tartan Farm. They met when Nafzger brought Fairway Phantom, a horse he trained to victories in the 1980 Breeders' Futurity and 1981 Arlington Classic, to Saratoga for the 1981 Travers. Nerud, who was then the president of Tartan Farm, was taken with Nafzger's work with Fairway Phantom, and asked him to manage a string at Arlington Park.

"John Nerud was my mentor in Thoroughbred racing," Nafzger said. "He taught me so much; he was like my father in the world of Thoroughbreds."

Around the same time that Nerud and Nafzger began working together, the Frances A. Genter Stable, a partner of Tartan, was looking to expand its operation with divisions around the country. Nafzger began training for the stable and developed Autumn Glitter, Coolawin, Orono, Star Choice, and Zero Minus into stakes winners for Mrs. Genter. In 1987, Tartan began dispersing horses, and Nerud recommended a Fappiano colt to Bentley Smith, Genter's son-in-law and the manager of the stable. The $70,000 weanling, who was later named Unbridled, became Nafzger's first Kentucky Derby winner.

Unbridled, a leggy and attractive bay colt with a white blaze dominating his face, began his career with a $10\frac{1}{2}$-length victory at Arlington Park, but didn't win another race at 2 until he took the $56,000 What a Pleasure at Calder on Christmas Eve. As a 3-year-old, he romped by four lengths in the Florida Derby, but finished third behind favored Summer Squall in his final Derby prep, the Blue Grass Stakes, and went off at odds of almost 11-1 at Churchill Downs.

Racing in 12th place after a half-mile, the big colt began to roll under jockey Craig Perret and was just a half-length off Summer Squall with a quarter of a mile to go. The stage was set for a "Hallmark moment" that was captured on national television as Nafzger gave Mrs. Genter a play-by-play of Unbridled's race. The 92-year-old Genter, whose eyesight was failing, stood close beside Nafzger, one of four trainers that ABC selected to wear a microphone in the hope that one of them would have the horse that wore the traditional blanket of roses in the winner's circle.

Unbeknownst to Nafzger, an ABC camera was also trained on him and Mrs. Genter. As the field swung into the stretch and Unbridled barreled past Summer Squall, Nafzger shouted, "He's taking the lead! Mrs. Genter, you're going to win the Kentucky Derby!" When Unbridled raced past the finish line, a 3½-length winner, Nafzger exclaimed, "You've won the Kentucky Derby, Mrs. Genter . . . I love you!" The elderly owner drew her left hand up to her face in disbelief. Her joy was undisguised.

Unbridled ran in each leg of the Triple Crown, finishing second to Derby runner-up Summer Squall in the Preakness and fourth in Go and Go's Belmont Stakes. He capped the season with a win over older horses in the Breeders' Cup Classic at Belmont Park, however, and was recognized as the champion 3-year-old, while Nafzger earned an Eclipse Award as that year's outstanding trainer.

Retired the following year after finishing fourth in the Classic, Unbridled entered the breeding shed with earnings of $4.4 million. He passed on his brilliance as a racehorse to a multitude of his progeny, including the Nafzger-trained Banshee Breeze, who won the 3-year-old filly championship in 1998 after taking the Grade 1 Alabama, Coaching Club American Oaks, and Spinster for owners James Tafel and Jayeff B Stables.

Among Unbridled's 38 stakes winners were Kentucky Derby winner Grindstone; Preakness winner Red Bullet; and Belmont Stakes winner Empire Maker. Unbridled was euthanized in October 2001 after suffering a severe case of colic.

Although Unbridled provided the Nafzgers with many glorious memories, one recollection that brings tears to Wanda's eyes is the thought of the colt's constant companion throughout his career, a lead pony named Mustard. When Carl asked his wife to tell the story, Wanda just shook her head and indicated that she was too choked up.

"Mustard was a pony horse," Nafzger said. "He died at 37 years old. We bought him off an Indian reservation in New Mexico, and Unbridled did not travel without Mustard. We have a picture from the Preakness of Mustard and Unbridled kissing. Unbridled had the traditional stall for the Derby winner at Pimlico, and I made sure that Mustard had the stall next to him. When they got there, they reached their noses together, and Unbridled gave him a smooch.

"Mustard went crazy when we turned him out and retired him at Ocala Stud Farm. It was sad, because every time a van drove in, Mustard ran to the fence, thinking he was going to be traveling, like he had with Unbridled."

Nafzger's approach to getting Unbridled to the Kentucky Derby in 1990 was different from the route he mapped out for his 2007 Derby winner, Street Sense. Unbridled prepped in four races as a 3-year-old before the Derby; Street Sense had only two.

"Unbridled needed the experience; Street Sense had already run against the best as a 2-year-old," Nafzger said of his contrasting methods with his Derby winners.

As a 2-year-old, Unbridled raced six times, but never against graded company. Street Sense, on the other hand, ran in three graded races in five starts at 2. The son of Street Cry finished third in both the Grade 3 Arlington-Washington Futurity and the Grade 1 Breeders' Futurity at Keeneland, and won the Breeders' Cup Juvenile by a record 10 lengths after coming from well off the pace at Churchill Downs.

Street Sense's victories in the 2006 Breeders' Cup Juvenile and the 2007 Kentucky Derby made him the first horse to win both races since the inaugural running of the Breeders' Cup in 1984, although believers in the "Juvenile Jinx" failed to take into account the fact that not all of those Juvenile winners actually ran in the next year's Derby; before Street Sense, only 13 winners of the Juvenile had entered the starting gate at Churchill Downs on the first Saturday in May. He also ended the drought of 2-year-old champions who came up short in Louisville by becoming the first colt since 1979 Derby winner Spectacular Bid to win the Eclipse Award at 2 and the Derby at 3.

Nafzger said his goal with Street Sense, who wintered as a 3-year-old at Palm Meadows Training Center in Boynton Beach, Florida, was to bring him to the Derby "fresh" and "dead fit." Until Street Sense, the last horse to win the Kentucky Derby with two or fewer preps at 3 was Sunny's Halo in 1983.

After a March 8 work, which was officially recorded as five furlongs in 1:01, Nafzger settled on the two-turn Tampa Bay Derby for Street Sense's first start as a 3-year-old. He said the timing of the March 17 Tampa Bay Derby "fell into the slot" as being the most attractive option for him after that workout. The Tampa Bay Derby was run 14 days before the Florida Derby. With Street Sense sitting on go, Nafzger didn't want to wait until the Gulfstream Park race to get the colt's sophomore campaign underway.

"The Tampa race worked with the [breeze] schedule we had him on, and he was right on target to run there," Nafzger said.

Street Sense won the 1¹⁄₁₆-mile Tampa Bay Derby by a nose over the favorite, Any Given Saturday. Aboard Street Sense was Calvin Borel, who rode the colt throughout his career.

"I worked Street Sense at Palm Meadows [March 8], and

Calvin flew in because it was a major work," Nafzger said. "I told Calvin I wanted a good work. I called Mr. Tafel right after the work, and I said, 'If he comes out of this work right, we are going to the Tampa Bay Derby.' All I needed then was a half-mile or five-eighths work and we could ship to Tampa. I didn't need any more time; I hadn't taken anything out of him. The horse just exploded that morning with Calvin. He looked like he was walking. We were going to Tampa Bay. We were ready.

"Our instructions to Calvin in the paddock at Tampa Bay were, 'Don't let Any Given Saturday get too far out; try to hook him up in the lane,'" Nafzger continued. "'He'll probably beat us because he had a race over the track, but we can't let our horse sit back there and come running down the lane and be second by four lengths. I've got to have a hard race.' I really thought we probably would get beat, but we would get the race, and bounce into the Blue Grass.

"When he won the Tampa Bay Derby, I told Mr. Tafel, 'If he keeps up this good, like I think he will, we got one hell of a shot. We'll win the Derby.' The Tampa Bay race put us right on target."

As he had done with Unbridled, Nafzger selected the Blue Grass at Keeneland as Street Sense's final Derby prep. The difference this time was that the Blue Grass, run three weeks before the Derby, would be contested over an artificial surface for the first time. As a 2-year-old, Street Sense finished third in the Breeders' Futurity on Keeneland's Polytrack, but that didn't deter Nafzger.

"I knew my horse would run on an artificial surface, even if he might not be his best on an artificial surface," he explained. "That didn't matter to me. I saw the fitness I got out of him running him at Keeneland in the Breeders' Futurity as a 2-year-old. To be fit enough to win the Derby, I had to have a hard race.

But I needed a real hard race where I could still bounce back in three weeks. The objective coming to the Derby was to have enough fitness and conditioning to win the race. After the Blue Grass, I would see if I would need light works or heavy works to bounce him to the Derby."

Another thing that appealed to Nafzger about the Blue Grass was that he didn't have to worry about bad weather affecting the Polytrack. As it turned out, a steady rain fell throughout most of the afternoon.

"I had to have a track that I could trust; and it didn't matter if it rained, poured, or what," Nafzger said.

In the bizarrely run Blue Grass, Street Sense finished second, beaten a nose by Dominican, who entered the race with two previous wins over Polytrack at Keeneland and Turfway Park. The early fractions were ridiculously slow for a 1⅛-mile stakes race—26.12 seconds for the opening quarter-mile, 51.46 for the half, and 1:16.65 for six furlongs. It was a mad dash to the wire after a mile in 1:39.82, and the final time was 1:51.33. Less than half a length separated the top four finishers in the race. In the stretch, Street Sense drifted in and squeezed Great Hunter, who finished fifth.

"We had that really odd race in the Blue Grass," Nafzger said. "Nobody wanted the lead. The speed ran 1:16 and change in a Grade 1. And then everyone ran home the fastest three-eighths [34.68] that you can imagine. We got beat. It wasn't because of the artificial surface. The horse made two mistakes. At the head of the lane, all he had to do was swing out and go. He dug back in behind Great Hunter, and then he came back out and back in, and then he got bumped. That bump didn't cost him the race. What cost Street Sense the race was his mistakes. By him ducking back behind Great Hunter twice, breaking his momentum, that little devil Street Sense never worked but three-eighths of a mile. See, it was Street Sense saying, 'I'm doing my own thing.'

"There are only three things I watch in a horse race. Did I make a mistake? Did the horse make a mistake? Did the jockey make a mistake? When you make mistakes, you get beat. Mistakes are not acceptable in Grade 1's."

It was a loss, but Nafzger didn't fret, and plotted a schedule that would have Street Sense work twice at Churchill Downs before the Kentucky Derby. The first move came on April 24, and was just what the trainer wanted: a sharp five furlongs in 59 seconds. The second breeze was May 1—the Tuesday of Derby Week—and Street Sense covered five furlongs in 1:01.

"The first breeze was a sharp five-eighths, since he did not run but three-eighths of a mile in the Blue Grass," Nafzger said. "The second five-eighths was to seat the screw."

He approached Street Sense's final works with the following in mind: "The first was to flush his system; the second was like a practice run—a dress rehearsal. The idea before the Derby was to let him do enough, have fun, relax, and want to do more in the race."

Nafzger achieved his goal: He had a fresh and fit horse for the Derby. Street Sense, who idled near the back of the 20-horse field, with only two horses beat after the opening half-mile, turned on the burners around the far turn, collared the pace-setting Hard Spun at the three-sixteenths pole, and powered to a 2¼-length win. Curlin finished third, 5¾ lengths behind Hard Spun.

It was Curlin who got the better of both Street Sense and Hard Spun in the Preakness, a race that validated the efforts of the top three finishers in the Derby. Curlin finished a head in front of Street Sense, with Hard Spun four lengths farther back in third.

In the Preakness, favored Street Sense wove his way through the field and blew by Curlin—who was to his outside—in upper stretch. Street Sense had a 1½-length advantage with a furlong remaining, but suddenly Curlin seemed to gain momentum, and he wore down the Derby winner in the final yards.

"After Street Sense got beat in the Preakness, everybody's saying, 'He got beat in the Preakness.' He didn't get beat in the Preakness. He stopped. He went to the lead, opened up, and went: 'Ha, I won this,'" said Nafzger, who believes that Street Sense thought the race was over, adding that his colt "is enough of a racehorse to keep running" when he is hooked by a challenger. If Street Sense thought the race was in the bag, so did his trainer.

"When Street Sense went by them so fast, I thought it was all over. It was a wonder I didn't head to the winner's circle. Then I saw Curlin coming back, and I said, 'Oh, crap.'"

Nafzger didn't waste time lamenting the outcome of the Preakness; rather, he began looking ahead to the rest of the season. With no Triple Crown on the line, he saw no sense in pounding away on his colt by running in the Belmont Stakes. Instead, the trainer plotted a course that would lead Street Sense to the Breeders' Cup Classic.

"You never second-guess," he said. "All we know is that he didn't win the Preakness. It took us about 10 days to decide to skip the Belmont. I said to Mr. Tafel, 'You love the Travers, and I love the Travers. Let's just head to the Travers.' So we did. We had already set the program to go to the Breeders' Cup Classic."

Street Sense won the Jim Dandy, his prep for the Travers, over a moderate field. Curlin and Hard Spun showed up in the more intriguing Haskell, which was won by Any Given Saturday. Hard Spun and Curlin took the second and third spots, respectively. The top three in the Haskell passed the Travers, although

Hard Spun was at Saratoga that day and won the seven-furlong King's Bishop, run 44 minutes before the $1 million "Midsummer Derby," which came up light in quality, aside from Street Sense.

Nafzger thought the main threat in the field of seven might be Sightseeing, who won the Peter Pan at Belmont by a nose in May and had finished third by 2¼ lengths to Street Sense in the Jim Dandy, rallying late and galloping out past the winner. Trainer Shug McGaughey, who had won previous runnings of the Travers with Easy Goer and Rhythm in 1989 and 1990 and with Coronado's Quest in 1998, had been targeting the Travers all summer, and on the Monday before the race, Nafzger told David Grening of *Daily Racing Form*, "I know how Shug can take a horse and build him up to a certain race, and I know Shug's been looking at this race. Sightseeing was closing really strong [in the Jim Dandy] and we got another eighth of a mile to go."

That last eighth of a mile was a thriller, but the challenge to Street Sense, the 1-4 favorite, did not come from Sightseeing; instead, it was 9-1 shot Grasshopper who ran the race of his life while making his stakes debut.

Under Robby Albarado, the regular rider of Curlin, Grasshopper took the lead heading into the first turn and held it down the backstretch, with Calvin Borel biding his time with Street Sense in third, 1½ lengths off the pace through six furlongs. Rounding the far turn, Street Sense began closing in, and as the two colts passed the quarter pole, they hooked up in a battle that lasted almost the length of the stretch.

Street Sense, who had taken the inside path to victory in the Breeders' Cup Juvenile and Derby, was on the outside this time, with Borel whipping right-handed. In the final yards, he hit Street Sense left-handed, and the colt edged clear by a half-length.

Borel did not want a repeat of the Preakness, in which Street Sense got lackadaisical after making the lead. He told Grening after the Travers, "When Curlin beat me I didn't have nothing to run at. Really and truly I was riding him [in the Travers], but at the same time I was trying to keep [Grasshopper] there as a target at all times till the last three or four jumps."

The Travers capped a tremendous week at Saratoga for Nafzger. He had won the previous weekend's Alabama with the Bentley Smith-owned Lady Joanne to become just the fifth trainer since 1901 to win both of those races in the same year. Not bad for a trainer in semi-retirement.

After finishing second to Hard Spun in the Kentucky Cup Classic, which was run over Turfway Park's Polytrack, Street Sense was set to make his final career start in the Breeders' Cup Classic at Monmouth Park. On the two earlier occasions that Street Sense had a prep race over Polytrack and lost, he had won his next starts: the Breeders' Cup Juvenile and the Kentucky Derby.

The Classic underscored the strength of that year's 3-year-old crop. It drew a field nine, with Street Sense favored at 5-2. Four of the first five choices in the betting were 3-year-olds, with only 4-year-old Lawyer Ron, who had just finished a neck behind Curlin in the Jockey Club Gold Cup at Belmont, given much consideration among the older horses. Lawyer Ron and Any Given Saturday were the co-second choices at just under 4-1, followed closely by Curlin.

Racing over a sloppy and sealed track, Curlin was much the best that day, winning by 4½ lengths over Hard Spun. Street Sense, who lacked the stretch acceleration he had shown in his previous races, finished fourth, one length behind the 28-1 Awesome Again. Street Sense was beaten a total of 9¼ lengths by Curlin, who was voted 3-year-old champion and Horse of the Year.

"It rained at the Classic and I guess that I got unlucky," Nafzger said. "Life goes on. Curlin was a hell of a horse. You know the biggest disappointment I had with Street Sense was finishing fourth in the Breeders' Cup Classic. You know why? It was the only time he ran less than third. But here is another reason. If we ran third in the Classic, the horses that had been one-two-three in the Derby and Preakness would have run one-two-three in the Classic. That would have been a first, and never would be repeated. If it was a dry track, I doubt there would have been 2½ lengths between me, Hard Spun, and Curlin in the Classic. Those three horses were unbelievable."

In 2008, Street Sense began stallion duties at Kentucky's Darley America, where his sire, Street Cry, also stands.

Nafzger said the 2007 Breeders' Cup was an indication that all racetracks should switch to synthetic surfaces. That opinion is not a popular one. Even most trainers who advocate the use of artificial tracks believe that conventional racing surfaces still have their place.

"The Breeders' Cup made me a great advocator of artificial surfaces," Nafzger said. "They need them everywhere. You got to put in as many common denominators as you can, and learn how to adapt to those denominators. We will learn how to train the horse for an artificial surface; we'll learn what kind of shoes they need; we'll learn how to ride them. But you have to take out as many variables as you can."

For Nafzger, part of the fun of training is getting to know the idiosyncrasies of each of his horses. He is fond of anthropomorphizing when talking about the horses that have come through his barn. And much like proud parents, Carl and Wanda, who have no children, absolutely delight in sharing tales about Unbridled and Street Sense, who were very different in demeanor.

"Unbridled was a gentle giant, and gave me confidence," Nafzger said. "He always looked at me as if to say, 'What are you worried about? I got it handled.'

"Street Sense was all about: 'I'll do my own thing. If Calvin asks me, I might change.' Otherwise, Street Sense trained you. You knew where you were with him all the time. With him, it was: 'You think that worked? That didn't work very good. Let's do my own thing.' He was a very independent horse. Street Sense was like: 'Okay, we'll play.' And the next minute he wanted you out of his stall. I used to play with him and all at once he got playing and then after five minutes, he decided that was enough."

Wanda said Borel and Street Sense had a deep connection; one of the strongest she has seen between horse and rider.

"Calvin and Street Sense had an unbelievable rapport," she said. "He loved Calvin. When Calvin got on him, he seemed to know that he had to perform."

Ian Wilkes said he always got a kick out of the stories told by Borel's fiancée, Lisa Funk, about how much the rider adored Street Sense. The colt was always on Borel's mind, whether he was awake or asleep.

"Calvin called Street Sense 'Big Daddy Rabbit,'" Wilkes said. "It was because of his big ears. Lisa said Calvin would be at home, riding the couch, and would say, 'C'mon, Big Daddy Rabbit.' She said that Calvin would be sound asleep and he would be dreaming and talking: 'Big Daddy Rabbit. Wait. Don't go yet.'"

The enthusiasm Nafzger exudes when talking about his horses is also apparent when he answers questions about the racing industry. He believes the industry as a whole is guilty of not putting the well-being of the horse first. One of Nafzger's peeves is the pressure from racetracks to fill races and produce full betting cards.

"Until we get back to the horse, we will not solve our problems," he said. "We've made the horse into a money-making vehicle for gambling. If you listen to track management, you hear, 'We need more racing dates. We need bigger fields. If you don't run that horse, you're not getting stalls next year.' Tracks have done as much to destroy the horse as anybody. They push the owner and trainer, and place the blame on them.

"Our racing secretaries now are basically controlled by management. There is no rhythm to the condition book. They will write anything to fill.

"Nowadays, the trainer is under [pressure] to hit 20 or 21 percent in wins. Nowadays, it's run, run, run. We run from one meet to the next. Six days a week. Hammer, hammer. Big fields. I pointed out to one track-management person that tracks want 10 horses per field for the gamblers. I said, 'Let's take 10 races, 10 horses, that's a hundred, six days of racing, and you got 600 horses. Your barn area holds 1,500 horses, so that means every horse has to run every two weeks.' Mathematically, it doesn't work.

"We all turn the horse into a vehicle of economics—the breeder, track management, the owners," he continued. "We have to get back to the horse. I don't know how that can be done. But the first thing we have to do is remove our wants and egos and greed. What if we put the horse first? The horse doesn't lie. He'll tell you if he isn't feeling well enough to run. 'My ankles are hurting, take me home and get me well.' What if we did that? What would it do to our breed and our racing? It would cause a whole major adjustment and then the horse would no longer be an economical vehicle. The horse is the most honest player in the world. You can dump a million dollars in his stall and all he is going to do is nibble on it and crap on it. That is what makes this game beautiful. The horse is racing.

And we need to get back to the horse."

For years, trainers have been outspoken about their desire for a uniform medication rule. The permissible level of a medication in New York might not necessarily be the legal threshold in Kentucky or Florida, or the drug might be allowed in one state, but not another. Penalties for violations are far from consistent, and vary from state to state. Since many of the top trainers in the country are represented by divisions in multiple locales, and ship horses to and from different racing jurisdictions, having a uniform medication rule would put everyone on the same page.

"First of all, years ago tracks should have started taking a percentage of the betting handle to fund testing," Nafzger said. "Medication is a necessity to training a racehorse, but in excess, it is stupidity. You can argue every point, and it is a kind of touchy subject, but I am for medication if we have established levels where the medication has a known effect. Then we can abide by those levels. We need a uniform medication rule with levels that substantiate its use. Then we can comply with the rule. I would love to have a uniform medication rule."

Nafzger said there is no "black magic" to training a racehorse. He approaches the conditioning of a horse not through force, which he said would bring resistance, but with fostering and encouragement so the animal does what comes naturally. He feels that one of the quickest ways to discourage a horse from realizing his full potential is to place him in a situation where he is incapable of performing at his best.

"If you take a horse and run him over his head, he'll try," he said. "The second time you run him over his head he'll try, but not as hard. The third time, the biggest fight you are going to have is getting him to the paddock, because he is not going to want to run. Now if you drop him to a $25,000 claimer off an allowance race, and he sits back there and comes running and beats a few horses, he will be: 'Wow, I'm getting good now.' Because he is in his class, and accomplishment builds confidence."

When it comes to preparing a horse to race, Nafzger looks to the horse to "tell him" the best method. If a particular strategy isn't benefiting a horse, Nafzger will make the necessary adjustments in the training routine until the horse is happy and willing to go about his work.

"What I did with the horse yesterday is very important," he said. "What I see today is going to tell me what I will do with him tomorrow. So it's a steady and slow process. It's not hard to train a racehorse. It's very hard to be patient."

Nafzger said he tells owners that the process of training horses is like building furniture.

"If you put the screw in too deep, you have to fill it with wax and that leaves a blemish," he said. "If you don't put it in far enough, you tear your shirt, or you hang stuff on it. But if you put it in really smooth, and the varnish goes over it, the screw itself becomes part of the beauty of the chair. So that is what you have to do with a horse. If you get him too tight in his training, he isn't going to run. If he isn't tight enough, he won't be able to finish.

"See, the thing about training is that you never quit learning. The day you quit learning is the day you become ignorant. The horse will teach you something every day. If you're around horses, you are still learning. And the beauty of it all is that the horse does not lie; we lie to ourselves, but the horse doesn't lie."

Something that demonstrates Nafzger's willingness to keep learning is his unconventional practice for cooling out horses, which he adopted in 1988: Rather than being led around by a hotwalker for the customary 30 to 45 minutes after a workout, each horse is given water, bathed, and brought into the stall, where it is rubbed down—much as a human athlete would receive a massage after a training session. Rubbing on a horse encourages circulation throughout the body, which promotes a feeling of well-being. It also establishes contact between the groom and horse, and Nafzger believes that connection is one of the most important elements of a horse's development.

"By rubbing on them, you bring blood to the surface," he said. "I was told when I started to do this that horses would tie up on me"—suffer muscle spasms due to a build-up of lactic acid—"but I found that happened a lot less or not at all. I think this method creates a better relationship between the human and the horse. It's really about having a horse establish contact with humans. Once they get into their stall, where they have their hay and water, the horse is ready to relax and let down."

Again and again, Nafzger returns to the topic of what goes on in the mind of a horse.

"Horses don't reason," he said. "Horses learn. So I train horses with the 'monkey in the tree' theory. I talked about that in a public-speaking engagement. I asked, 'How many people here would like to train a Kentucky Derby horse?' Of course, everybody was eager to hear that and said, 'Yeah, yeah, yeah.' It's a very simple theory: You lead a horse under a tree. The monkey jumps on his back. The horse doesn't go back under the tree after that, but what he doesn't know is that the zookeeper caught the monkey and took him back to the zoo. Whatever you teach them, they learn. The horse is a by-product of what you teach him."

Nafzger believes horses convey their state of mind through their demeanor, and are anxious to please.

"You know what tickles me the most about horses?" he asked. "It is how much they really, really understand. I know they are considered dumb; not as smart as pigs. This is all philosophy

CARL NAFZGER

VITAL STATISTICS

CATEGORY	STS.	W%	ROI
180+Trn	3	0	0
61-180Trn	11	0.27	3.89
2nd45-180Lay	9	0.11	0.98
2nd180+Lay	2	0	0
1-7Last	1	0	0
1stStart	7	0	0
2ndMdn	6	0	0
MSWtoMCL	3	0.33	3.4
1stTurf	3	0	0
1stBlink	3	0	0
1stLasix	5	0	0
2YO	7	0	0
Dirt/Turf	3	0	0
Turf/Dirt	6	0	0
BlinkOn	3	0	0
BlinkOff	2	0	0
Sprint/Route	7	0.14	0.63
Route/Sprint	5	0	0
31-60Days	27	0.07	0.7
WonLast	10	0.1	0.92
Wet	5	0.2	1.04
Dirt	34	0.15	0.97
Turf	27	0.11	1.6
Sprints	32	0.06	0.44
Routes	48	0.15	1.47
MCL	5	0.4	2.92
MSW	33	0.03	0.12
Claim	8	0.25	1.72
ALW	22	0.14	1.04
STK	9	0.11	3.29
GSTK	6	0.17	4.93
DebutMCL	1	0	0
Synth	19	0.05	0.45
Turf/Synth	5	0	0
Synth/Turf	4	0	0

*January 1, 2008, through February 8, 2009, North American runners only

CAREER HIGHLIGHTS

BREEDERS' CUP

STARTS	1ST	2ND	3RD
18	2	3	1

WINNERS
Unbridled: Classic (1990)
Street Sense: Juvenile (2006)

TRIPLE CROWN

STARTS	1ST	2ND	3RD
8	2	2	1

WINNERS
Unbridled: Kentucky Derby (1990)
Street Sense: Kentucky Derby (2007)

ECLIPSE AWARDS
Leading Trainer (1990)
Unbridled: 3-Year-Old Colt (1990)
Banshee Breeze: 3-Year-Old Filly (1998)
Street Sense: 2-Year-Old Colt (2006)

RECORDS/NOTABLE ACHIEVEMENTS
Inducted into racing Hall of Fame (2008).

Became the first trainer to win the Kentucky Derby with the Breeders' Cup Juvenile winner (Street Sense).

Inducted into the Texas Horse Racing Hall of Fame in 2007.

Tied for leading trainer at Keeneland's fall meet in 1994.

CAREER SUMMARY

STS.	1ST	2ND	3RD	EARNINGS
8,122	1,077	1,071	1,085	$50,623,188

*Through February 8, 2009, North American runners only

145

now. Their intelligence, their brains, may not make them smart, but I think their emotional side is even stronger [than some other animals]. They are more like a dog. They want to please. I've had horses look me in the eye with: 'Whose stupid idea was it to put me in this race?'"

Chances are, if horses could talk, Nafzger's would be praising him for "listening" to them.

Seven

Todd Pletcher

Perhaps the most successful trainee ever to emerge from the shed row of Hall of Famer D. Wayne Lukas is not a horse, but Todd Pletcher. While Lukas took the concept of running a multidivisional stable to a new level in the 1980s, shipping his horses wherever he thought they could win, Pletcher has close to 250 horses in five divisions around the country and set single-season earnings records three years in a row. Lukas launched unprecedented attacks on Triple Crown and Breeders' Cup races, setting a Cup record in 1987 by running 14 horses in one day, including five in the Juvenile Fillies. Pletcher surpassed that mark in 2006 with 17 starters. Lukas is the all-time leading winner of Breeders' Cup races, with 18. Pletcher can't match that tally yet, but give him a few years. In 1996, his old boss told *The New York Times*, "He's going to break every record I've ever held."

In 1995, Pletcher was 28 and working

as an assistant in Lukas's New York division, based at Belmont Park. He had been with Lukas for nearly seven years, and while he considered himself lucky to be working shoulder to shoulder with one of the most prolific trainers of racing's modern era, surrounded by a multitude of outstanding horses, the time had come to start his own operation.

Pletcher, a son of a horse trainer, gave the decision careful consideration.

"I thought about it a lot," he said. "I think sometimes when you are an assistant, you think an opportunity is just going to present itself and that someone is going to call you up one day and say, 'I would like you to train the best horses in the world.' After a while, you realize that is probably unlikely to happen. For me, I just thought it was time to give it a try."

Actually, someone did call Pletcher, and although that person was not a big owner himself, he knew people who were. Bloodstock agent Mike Ryan phoned and said he would send Pletcher some clients if he went out on his own.

"That was the little bit of the push I needed," said Pletcher. "My dad had horses in partnership with a lady called Betty Massey and I got those horses. I had enough at least to put something behind some webbings, and put my name out there and try to get going."

Pletcher left Lukas in December 1995 and set up shop for the winter at Hialeah Park, where he was given 20 stalls. Initially, only seven were occupied, but the empty ones weren't vacant for long. Besides Massey, Pletcher's initial owners—all of whom he still trained for in 2008—were Stuart and Anita Subotnick, Robert Clay of Three Chimneys Farm, and Victor and Ramona DiVivo, whose Majestic Number was Pletcher's first career winner at Gulfstream Park in February 1996.

Pletcher's rise in racing was meteoric. Just six years after saddling his first winner, he trained Left Bank to an Eclipse Award as champion older male of 2002. In 2004 at Lone Star Park, he won his first Breeders' Cup races with Ashado (the Distaff) and Speightstown (the Sprint). Both horses earned Eclipse Awards that year, as did Pletcher; his first of four consecutive titles.

More Eclipse Awards followed for Pletcher-trained horses. Ashado earned another in 2005. In subsequent years, Pletcher added to his already dazzling resume by claiming year-end championships with English Channel, Fleet Indian, Lawyer Ron, Rags to Riches, and Wait a While.

The trainer established North American single-year earnings records in 2005 and 2006, with $20,882,842 and $26,820,243, respectively, in purse money. He eclipsed his own record yet again in 2007 when his runners accumulated $28,111,697.

There was never a time that Pletcher, a native of Dallas, didn't consider becoming a trainer. As a kid, he worked alongside his father, Jake "J.J." Pletcher, a Quarter Horse and Thoroughbred trainer, at tracks in the West, South, and Midwest. At the insistence of his parents, he went to college, but he wasn't going to stray too far from the world of racing. He attended the University of Arizona's Race Track Industry Program, graduating with a degree in animal science.

During summer breaks from school, Pletcher worked for trainers Henry Moreno and Charlie Whittingham, and Lukas. After college, in 1989, he came into Lukas's employ full-time. Lukas, who would join the Hall of Fame 10 years later, ran an operation that focused on quality, a staggering number of horses, and far-flung divisions, all managed with machinelike precision.

Not surprisingly, when the time came for Pletcher to go his own way, he followed the same business model. During the summer of 2008, Pletcher said he had 240 horses in training, with five divisions spread across the country. Depending on the time of the year, he has operations in New York, California, Kentucky, Illinois, Florida, and New Jersey.

"Usually around June of every year, we peak out at slightly higher [numbers]," Pletcher said. "You get 2-year-olds in April, May, and June, and by the time July rolls around, you have some with shins or various other things and you need to stop on them. I would say the highest number is generally in June.

"It's kind of been a steady growth," he continued. "I started off December of 1995 with seven, and by the time we left Hialeah [the following spring] it was up to around 20. I think the next step was a second division where we sent horses to Churchill. So we got up to the 60-to-80 range. Then 100. It seemed like we went from 100 to 200 quickly; it just happened. It took maybe six or seven years to get up to that 100 level, and then it got up to 200 quickly."

In the 1980s, Lukas, who has trained a record 24 horses to earn Eclipse Awards and has saddled the winners of 13 Triple Crown races, broke new ground in the sport when he success-fully expanded his operation to multiple locales without sacrificing the quality of the stable. Pletcher was extremely fortunate to gain firsthand knowledge of how such an expansive operation can be run smoothly and profitably. His tenure with Lukas was akin to someone obtaining a degree at a top business school.

"Wayne was great at being able to set up an organization," Pletcher said. "Before him, trainers were afraid to expand beyond one barn or one location. Wayne ran his training operation like a corporation or a business. Once our stable grew beyond a certain point, knowing how he did that was helpful. It allowed us to expand and yet still be able to manage it. Obviously, Wayne is a terrific caretaker of his horses. He always emphasizes how his horses look. Always has the best of everything—the best equipment, straw, feed, and tries to emphasize quality. I think we have tried to incorporate some of those things."

Pletcher acknowledged that there had been other trainers who operated multiple divisions, such as Hall of Famer Jack Van Berg; nevertheless, he considers Lukas a pioneer in that area.

"There were guys like Van Berg that did it too, and maybe he opened it up a little bit. But Wayne was really the one that I think sort of it made it okay that you could have a large operation without being the groom and the night watchman. I think before that, [owners] thought, 'If you are training my horse, you are supposed to be with the horse all the time.' There is some merit to that, but there's also some merit to the way we do it."

Lukas and his son, Jeff, who worked as his father's main assistant while Pletcher was in the barn, ran a disciplined operation. Their stables were always flawlessly maintained and beautifully manicured, which is still true today. There is never a stray piece of straw in the shed row. The horses are impeccably turned out, whether training or racing. Lukas himself cuts a dapper figure, whether he is wearing Wrangler jeans and a crisp shirt in the barn or a tailored suit in the paddock.

Pletcher has incorporated the same style of dress into his working routine, and his pristine barn is probably cleaner than most houses. The ubiquitous and trend-setting white bridles that have always made a Lukas runner easy to spot are another trademark of the Pletcher operation.

Pletcher, who broke Lukas's 1987 record of 92 stakes wins in a single season in 2006, with 100 winners, said he appreciated the discipline that was required of him while he was employed by Lukas.

"I didn't find Wayne difficult to work for," he said, adding,

"Jeff was sort of my mentor, and I was fortunate enough to work with him for the most part. They were demanding, but fair. I really enjoyed working with Jeff because he was really thorough and demanding. He was like a coach that made you a better player. He would get you on your toes and focused."

Pletcher said maintaining multiple divisions provides his owners with the option of moving their horses to a circuit at which they can be competitive, without changing trainers. It's a scenario that is also beneficial to him.

"If we have a horse here that needs to run at Philadelphia or Monmouth or Delaware, we have the capabilities to do that," he explained. "So I think that is actually helpful to the owners. I think a lot of times owners want to find a trainer and have a relationship with him and keep the horse in that organization, so it's an advantage to them."

When dealing with owners, diplomacy is a must for trainers. Pletcher said he never wants to give a client false hope about a horse's ability, and is totally candid when a move to a less competitive venue is in order.

"We try to be fairly straightforward about what we think the capabilities of a horse are," he said. "If anything, we underestimate. I don't try to tell my owners that this is 'a really good horse' until I think I really know that. I try to be extremely honest with what I think their value is.

"I'm sure a lot of times, they don't want to hear it. I don't want it to be that way, but they have an economic investment at stake, and I think it is my obligation to make sure they are aware of what they have."

Given Pletcher's high volume of runners, there are many instances when he has two or more horses—campaigned by different owners—aiming for the same race. Trying to keep everyone happy can be a challenge, but Pletcher said his edict of putting the horses first is a helpful guide to spotting his runners.

"There are certain situations where you can't keep them sep-arated," Pletcher said. "The big races are the obvious ones: Triple Crown races, the Breeders' Cup races. Generally, none of my clients have a problem with that.

"Occasionally, you run into a situation where some owner expects you to take another owner's horse and run it somewhere else, instead of against theirs. It has caused me problems at times, but I try to always put the horse first, and hopefully the rest of it falls into place. So the first thing I always try to do is what's best for the horse. Usually if you do that, everything else will take care of itself. There are situations certainly where it is in my best interests to run two horses in two different $100,000 races, as opposed to both horses in one $100,000 race. But again, I will try to do what is always best for the horse and the owner."

In an operation the size of Pletcher's, the staff is an important component, and his weekly payroll is massive—around $100,000 for his 200 employees. Candidates for a managerial position in Pletcher's stable need not apply if they are not pre-pared to spend long hours in the barn, as does the trainer him-self.

"I think for the most part all of our assistants have fallen into a similar category in terms of age; most of them are between 25 and 35," Pletcher said. "Obviously, they have to be willing to dedicate pretty much every waking moment to be at work. Some of the people have been promoted within the organiza-tion, and some have come from outside the organization. The profile is generally fairly clean-cut, young, energetic, and enthu-siastic about racing."

With more than 100 owners, good communication skills are essential for keeping Pletcher's clients in the loop. Although he has an office staff to help, he is very hands-on with his owners. Walk into Pletcher's office after training hours and it's less than even money that he will be on the phone with an owner. No sooner does he conclude a conversation than another incoming call requires his attention.

"We use fax, e-mail, and the phone to keep everyone aware," Pletcher said. "We have a weekly report that basically covers every horse and gives a recap of what happened last week and what we are planning on. It's short, to the point, with work-schedule information and upcoming races.

"My contact really depends upon what the owners need," he explained. "I've got some guys that I talk to six days a week. And I've got guys that I talk to six times a year. Sometimes it doesn't matter the number of horses I have for them. I might have 20 horses for one guy that I never talk to and one horse for some-one else who I talk to a lot."

Pletcher racks up plenty of frequent-flyer miles, and puts his Mercedes SUV to good use. A typical week involves visiting multiple locations, often two in the same day. He is based at Belmont Park, and Saratoga is a regular destination when the track is open for off-season training. Many of Pletcher's devel-oping 2-year-olds are stabled there when the race meeting is not in progress.

"The travel varies by season," he said. "Obviously, from April to November, it's a lot. It's pretty rare during that period that I am not going somewhere at least once a week. Normally what I would do, say on a Monday or a Tuesday, is get up, leave the house by 4:00, be at Monmouth by 5:15. Train there, leave there, and drive to Saratoga. Train the next day at Saratoga and maybe spend two or three days there, because of the volume of horses. And come back to New York, and then maybe fly to Churchill and then to Arlington."

Because it would be impossible for Pletcher to see each of his horses every day, there is a premium on daily communication between the trainer and his key staff members. Each division has a similar "playbook" in place.

"When you go to any of our organizations, basically the same things are happening at each of them," Pletcher said. "Start between 4:30 and 5:00. Each location has at least one assistant trainer and one if not two foremen, depending upon the number of horses we have in that location. Foremen are coming to work and checking a horse's feed tub, taking the temperatures of each horse, and putting that down on a chart. They do that each morning and afternoon.

"What we normally do then, at 10:00 or 10:30, after I have entered horses, we go over the training chart. We talk about what that horse did today, and what that horse will do tomorrow. Some of that is very routine. The horse galloped today, and will gallop tomorrow. Other times, you obviously have problems. You've got this and that and you need to talk about it. By doing that, it allows me to know exactly what these horses are doing each and every day. It also makes the assistants accountable for knowing what the horses are doing today and tomorrow, and reporting it back to me. It's a good system because we all are informed, and we know what is going on. Essentially, that is how I keep up with it."

According to Pletcher, the two most crucial times to evaluate a horse's soundness are when it breaks into a jog from a walk and when it comes back to a jog from a gallop. With a brigade of horses going to the track to train, it is sometimes difficult to monitor each horse as it makes those transitions. So, a morning ritual in the Pletcher barn is for every horse to jog—before going to the track to train—for the inspection of the trainer or his assistants.

"The one thing we have developed over the course of the years was to more effectively manage a larger number of horses at one location," Pletcher said. "We check all the legs and jog all the horses before they go to the track. Hopefully, by doing that we are maybe picking up on some subtle things, which might prevent us going out there to train and overexercising in a situation where there is a very slight injury.

"Especially at Palm Meadows [Training Center] and Saratoga, we might have 10 to 15 horses in a set, and this one jogs off to the right, and this one is going the other way. You can only see so many of them start off. So by jogging them at the barn before they go to the track, you can detect any issues. The two most important times you are really watching a horse train are those first few strides and those last few strides. That is generally when you are going to pick up on some issues. If there is a problem, they are going to show it right then."

As if keeping tabs on all his horses at various locations weren't enough, Pletcher also frequently attends sales of yearlings and 2-year-olds in training. Many of his owners acquire horses at auction, and he estimated that in 2008, 60 percent of the horses in his barn had been bought at sales.

Over the years, Pletcher has a demonstrated a deft touch with juveniles. Among his 2-year-old Grade 1 winners—who also were Grade 1 winners in subsequent seasons—were More Than Ready, Scat Daddy, and Ashado, all of whom were purchased at auction as yearlings.

When Pletcher inspects young horses at sales, he is more likely to focus his attention on conformation than the catalogue page.

"I'm probably more of a conformation guy first," he said. "Then I try to make a case for the pedigree—as opposed to the other way around. We go there looking for individuals and athletes and probably are a little bit overcritical of conformation in terms of correctness and those kind of things. I think because of that, a larger percentage of horses that we are responsible for are more likely to make the races and maybe have sounder careers. But I think you have to have an open enough mind to not say that you can't accept any horse that is offset in its knees. You have to put the whole picture together.

"I'm pretty critical of broodmares that have bad produce records," Pletcher added. "I would much rather have a maiden mare than a mare that's 0 for 5 or 0 for 6."

Pletcher has the luxury of training for a plethora of owners with deep pockets. One such owner is Englishman Michael Tabor, who sold the Arthur Prince chain of betting shops to Coral in the United Kingdom for $50 million in the mid-1990s. In a 2008 list compiled by London's *The Sunday Times*, Tabor was ranked the 134th-richest man in Britain, with a fortune estimated at $1.24 billion.

It was Tabor and his partners, John Magnier and Derrick Smith, who made the infamous purchase of The Green Monkey, whose $16 million sales price was a world record for a 2-year-old training in 2006. The colt, who was turned over to Pletcher after he was bought, worked a scorching 9.80 seconds for an eighth of a mile during a breeze show prior to the Fasig-Tipton Calder sale.

The Green Monkey, a son of Forestry, didn't race as a 2-year-old because of a pulled gluteal muscle. When he made it to the races as a 3-year-old, he never displayed any brilliance; the best he managed was a third and a pair of fourth-place finishes from three starts. The Green Monkey, who was retired in February 2008, now stands at Tabor and Magnier's Ashford Stud in Kentucky.

"We were always a little bit surprised that he wasn't training as well for us as he did when he was purchased at the Calder sale," Pletcher said. "I saw his work there and it was brilliant. Obviously, it was an eighth of a mile, but he did gallop out really well. We never saw the same speed for us that he displayed at Calder."

Many of Pletcher's 2-year-olds are broken at his father's farm in Ocala, Florida. He said the horses that are given their pre-racetrack education by his father are typically assessed in December of their yearling year or shortly after they officially turn 2 on January 1.

"Generally, our strategy, at least with the horses my dad breaks, is fairly early on, maybe December or January, we identify which ones are maybe slated to come early, like March 1," Pletcher said. "We sort of break them down with March 1, April 1, May 1, and June 1 as target dates that they might come into the racetrack. Obviously, you have to be extremely flexible with that schedule, but that is sort of what my dad is thinking as he develops them; maybe picking out a handful that are going to be ready at Keeneland in the spring. Those horses we'll get into my barn let's say March 1 in Florida. Believe it or not, with those we can get a pretty accurate line on how precocious they are and how they might run at that early stage. When you are only going 4½ furlongs, the criteria is different than for the ones you get later in the summer."

Pletcher said a good barometer for evaluating the ability of a juvenile is how the horse does when it breezes beyond a half-mile.

"My rule of thumb is I reserve judgment until they have gone a good five-eighths," he said. "The reason I say that is because I think most horses are capable of going a pretty good three-eighths or a pretty good half. That five-eighths barrier seems to separate the pretenders from the real ones."

No matter what the horse's age is, Pletcher will judge the work on the whole. He said the final time, which is part of a horse's past performances, might not always tell the tale of the work.

"If people looked at our work tabs a lot, they would say, 'There isn't a lot of variety in it.' There are a lot of half [miles] and five-eighths, and occasionally some three-quarters, but really what we have found to be the key with most of these works is what they do after the finish line. The ones that go five-eighths in 1:01—that might look great—but if they gallop out three-quarters in 1:17, to us that is a poor work. If they go 1:01 and then they go out in 1:14 and out seven-eighths in 1:28 or 29, now we know we've got a fit horse.

"A half in 49 can be totally different for one that goes off in 22 and finishes in 27; that is a horrible 49. Conversely, if they go off in 25-and-change and finish in 23-and-change and gallop out well, that is good work," he explained. "A lot of it is about observation. I think as a trainer, you develop a program through trial and error that works for you. Yes, you have to treat them all as individuals and do what works for that particular horse, but basically it all falls into sort of a general plan. In some ways it is a very complicated game, but in some ways it's a very basic game. I think when you try to get too creative that doesn't work."

As a rule, Pletcher said, turf horses can get away with a little less training.

"Take a horse like English Channel, even though he was a mile-and-a-half specialist, if you look at his work tab, very seldom, or if ever, did he work over five-eighths. Even though he had plenty of space between many of his races, he almost always breezed a half on the turf. But it might be deceiving if someone was just looking at his work tab where he breezed a half in 50, because he would gallop out another half in 50 or 52."

Pletcher said he has learned to stick with what works for him and not get caught up in overanalyzing how his rivals are preparing their horses, particularly before a major race.

"There is a little bit of a temptation there when you are leading up to big races, especially when you are in a Breeders' Cup or a Kentucky Derby situation, when everyone comes together, and you see the other horses," he said. "You might think, 'Oh, this horse worked this far and that fast.' I think what you really try is to stay focused on exactly what has worked for you in the past and what has worked for that specific horse and not worry about Bob Baffert's horse going in 58 or this horse going in 1:02. We approach it as: This is what we do and this is what works for us the rest of the year to get to there. So you try not to change what works for you and your horse. What works for you and your horse might not work for someone else. Everyone develops their own training patterns and methods. Some guys work fast, some guys work slow, others longer, shorter, what have you. You just focus on your own."

Through 2008, that focus had yet to produce a Kentucky Derby victory for Pletcher, who had sent out 21 horses in the race since his first attempt in 2000. Many trainers wait for decades to get to the Derby, and when they finally do, it's with just one horse; Pletcher had been training for less than five years when he took his first shot, bringing four starters to Churchill Downs. In 2006, he again ran four horses, with Bluegrass Cat giving the trainer his second runner-up finish in the race. (Invisible Ink was second in 2001.) In 2007, he saddled a record-tying five runners, but none of them finished in the money.

Those kinds of numbers cannot fail to draw attention, and every year around Derby time, at least one reporter writes an article pondering Pletcher's Derby dearth—something he thinks is "a little bit blown out of proportion because we ran five one year, four another year. It's not like we have been trying for 25 years to win the Derby.

"It's a very hard race to win," he mused. "I think more than anything . . . I don't think we have brought the right horse there at the right time."

Pletcher went on to say that part of the reason he has run so many horses in the Derby is simply that so many of them have done well leading up to it.

"Some of that is good placement; sending horses to the right races, the right Illinois Derby or the right Arkansas Derby, or the right graded races along the way to get them to the Derby. But I don't know that we have ever shown up with a horse on the day that was really, really the right horse for the Derby," he said.

Bandini might have been "the right horse" in 2005, but he chipped an ankle during the race and finished 19th.

"He was probably the most qualified for the Derby," said Pletcher. "He had the right breeding, running style, and all those things. But we probably ran a lot of horses that weren't good enough or couldn't go that far, or what have you. If you put your thumb over the first-place record, we've done okay with seconds and thirds. Frankly, a lot of our horses have over-achieved in the Derby."

Although Pletcher's hair is prematurely gray, it's likely that genetics, not Derby angst, is the cause.

"I know it sounds untrue, but I really don't sit back and stew on the whole Derby record that much," he said. "When it's over, it's over. Believe me, I want to win it, I would love to win it. But it doesn't gnaw at me. It doesn't bother me that it hasn't happened. In some ways, I think it is good. It gives us something out there to shoot for."

Any handicapper would probably take a short price that Pletcher will win the Derby someday. He already has a Belmont Stakes victory to his credit, courtesy of the filly Rags to Riches, who beat 2007 Preakness winner and eventual Horse of the Year Curlin by a head after a truly classic stretch duel in the 1½-mile race. Rags to Riches was only the third filly to win the Belmont, and the first to do so in 102 years.

Bought at auction by Michael Tabor and Derrick Smith for $1.9 million as a yearling, Rags to Riches entered the Belmont with wins in three Grade 1 races: the Las Virgenes, Santa Anita Oaks, and Kentucky Oaks. Her sire, A.P. Indy, had won the 1992 Belmont, and her dam, Better Than Honour, had produced the 2006 Belmont winner, Jazil, so Pletcher knew his filly had the pedigree to get the distance—but he didn't want ambition to override prudence.

"I kind of wrestled with what the right thing to do was," Pletcher said. "I knew she was a very special filly. She had already proven that to us. So what I was kind of torn between was, do I protect her and play it safe, and run her against strictly 3-year-old fillies as long as I can? Or do we take a shot at the really big prize? So it just kind of came down to gut reaction. We thought she was doing well and it was time to take a shot, and she was bred to go a mile and a half. But you go through this whole process trying to figure out what the right move is."

For a nanosecond after the field of seven left the starting gate in the Belmont, Pletcher rued his decision to run. Breaking from the outside under Pletcher's go-to rider, John Velazquez, Rags to Riches stumbled at the start. Photographs show the filly's nose as far down as the knees of the horse to her left, Hard Spun.

"When she stumbled out of the gate right at the start, the first thing that went through my mind was, I wrestled with the decision for the last couple of weeks, and it's all gone in one stride," Pletcher recalled. "Then she sort of recovered and put herself in position, and everything is going along pretty well. Then they turned for home, and you think this might really happen. Then Curlin starts to dig back. So many emotions are going through your mind in such a short period of time. Then when she finally won . . . My biggest thrill would be Rags to Riches winning the Belmont."

Rags to Riches would race only once again, in the Gazelle Stakes at Belmont in September. She finished second, beaten a half-length by Lear's Princess, and exited the race with a hairline fracture in her right front pastern. She was put back in training for a 4-year-old campaign, but the injury flared up again, and Pletcher announced Rags to Riches' retirement in March 2008.

"I knew it was coming for a little while before it happened," Pletcher said. "We tried to give her every chance to make it back, but in some ways it was more of a relief. You get to the point . . . she had accomplished so much and it was going to be hard to accomplish any more if she wasn't as good [physically] as she had been. There was no pressure from the owners to make it back. They were great. Everyone wanted to do what was best for her."

Rags to Riches was a favorite around the barn, but as much as Pletcher and his staff would miss her, emoting is not something he is known for. Even after the toughest beat, he displays an unruffled demeanor with reporters. He is articulate and polite and especially patient with journalists who unwittingly ask the same question that he answered for someone else five minutes earlier. Visitors to his barn will observe a comfortable yet professional relationship between him and his staff.

Calm, cool, and in control is Pletcher.

"Don't get me wrong, I have high moments and low moments, I just try not to show it on the surface," he said. "There is no way you can be in this business without having bad days and good days. That is the way it is. If you are going to be in it for the long haul, you have to keep that even keel and know that there are going to be some days you hate and some days where things are better than they seem.

"I never really felt that confrontations are productive. You go screaming at someone . . . I never really felt like it helps. I've tried it a few times to see what it was like and it really didn't help," he said, laughing. "I end up feeling bad or wishing I hadn't said something, so I just try to keep the even keel."

Although Pletcher is unlikely to say anything too radical or provocative during interviews, he possesses a dry sense of humor. When asked if he ever turned down an owner's offer to put horses in his barn, he dead-panned, "Sheikh Mohammed called yesterday and I said it wasn't a good time."

Not surprisingly, he has a cool-headed "wait and see" attitude concerning the proliferation of synthetic tracks in recent years. Although he won the 2008 spring training title at Keeneland, which features Polytrack, that did not make him a cheerleader for synthetic surfaces.

"Really, until they are around for 10 years or so, how are we going to know until we have enough data and evidence, and know how to maintain them?" Pletcher asked. "We are becoming more comfortable with them. But I think everyone wanted to rush to judgment and put them in all over the place without really knowing enough about them."

He is, however, outspoken when discussing a topic that is of paramount importance to trainers: the need for a uniform medication rule in each racing jurisdiction in the United States. It is a concept that many in the industry, particularly horsemen, would like to see realized. Withdrawal times, permissible levels of medications, and penalties for medication infractions now vary from state to state. The one thing all states have in common is the trainer-responsibility rule, also known as the absolute-insurer rule, which declares that the trainer is ultimately accountable for whatever offense occurs, even if it is through no fault of his own.

Pletcher would like to see a nationwide reform of medication rules, but conceded, "Maybe the only way to do that is to have no race-day medication, like they do in Europe and Dubai. Here we need the same rules for New York and California, and everywhere in between.

"But 'no medication' shouldn't be confused with 'zero tolerance,'" he continued. "That is a very different subject." He explained that without allowable threshold levels for some medications, there would be many "positives" resulting from trace levels, known as contamination cases.

Pletcher said he was the victim of a contamination case that occurred in 2004, when a minute amount (1.6 nanograms) of mepivacaine—a local anesthetic—was detected in one of his horses, Tales of Glory, after a win at Saratoga. He appealed the ruling of the New York State Racing and Wagering Board, but began serving a 45-day suspension in December 2006 after a state appellate court upheld the board's decision.

"It was a contamination issue; there absolutely was no history of the horse receiving that," he said. "I was used as an example. During my litigation, [the NYSRWB] changed the withdrawal time from seven days to four days."

The mepivacaine positive was the trainer's first. In 2008, another of his runners, Wait a While, tested positive for procaine after finishing third in the Breeders' Cup Filly and Mare

Turf at Santa Anita. Procaine, a local anesthetic, is a component of the penicillin shots Pletcher said Wait a While received after developing a fever two days after her victory in the Yellow Ribbon Stakes at Santa Anita on September 27. In a prepared statement following the public release of the California Horse Racing Board complaint against Pletcher in December 2008, the trainer said that he was advised by his veterinarians that 14 days "was more than ample withdrawal time" for the procaine to clear the filly's system. He said Wait a While was last treated with the antibiotic on October 6. The Filly and Mare Turf was run October 24. As of mid-February 2009, no further information regarding the CHRB's December complaint had been released.

In 2008, spurred by growing public concern about the welfare of racehorses—and a fear of governmental interference—the majority of racing jurisdictions in the United States adopted new rules concerning the use of anabolic steroids. Pletcher, who said he had already stopped giving steroids to his horses well in advance of those restrictions, believes that one of the reasons the topic sparked such controversy is that most people do not differentiate between the use of steroids in humans and horses.

"I think if you talk to veterinarians in general, most of them will tell you that anabolic steroids have a different effect on horses than humans," he said in June 2008. "I think most of the human athletes that are using them have very specific goals in mind: trying to build muscle mass, get bigger, get stronger, run faster, hit the ball farther, and all those things. Whereas the dosages used in horse racing, by responsible people, are not for promoting bigger muscles, necessarily, but to improve recovery time [between races] and appetite.

"Don't get me wrong, I'm sure there are trainers out there that abuse steroids and give dosages that are irresponsible," he said. "But for the trainers who are using them the correct way, there are certainly benefits to steroids. But if you put the idea out there that we are giving horses steroids, the public has been programmed to see Barry Bonds, Mark McGwire, and Sammy Sosa. It's probably just the wrong perception for our game. You basically have two ways of dealing with that. You either have to try to educate the public to what it really is, or you have to get rid of steroids. I think with everything going on in our industry right now, the simplest thing to do is to just get rid of them.

"I think they will still be used therapeutically. But personally, I probably won't use them at all just because I don't want to put myself in a position where I have to worry about a 30-day withdrawal versus a 31-day withdrawal, or whatever.

"There are a number of medications we don't use because of that," he added, citing clenbuterol, a bronchodilator, as an example. "I think it is very widely used, but we don't use it because I don't want to lay awake at night worrying that someone gave it 72 hours out instead of 96 hours out, by accident."

Pletcher is well aware that his high win percentage, which averages 22 percent since he began training, arouses suspicion in some quarters of the racing industry. In June 2008, he was winning at 22 percent for the year.

"To me that is one of the most frustrating things we deal with," he said. "You hear the innuendos and whatever. That is very frustrating because we work very hard at what we do and put a lot into it. The only thing I can say is just look at it over the long period.

"You see certain situations where some outfits do well over a short period of time. But to me, the guys that do it consistently, year after year after year . . . If you look at our statistics, even though our earnings are down [in 2008], we are still batting 22 percent in wins, and we're missing the Any Given Saturdays,

English Channels, Lawyer Rons, and Scat Daddys, who are
retired and were bringing our earnings up there when they
were in the barn. But our win percentage is consistent with
where it has been over the last 12 years. That would be my argu-
ment. We have proven ourselves many times, over and over
again."

That figure of 22 percent had dropped to 19 by the end of the
season, dipping below 20 percent for the first time since 2000.
For someone with Pletcher's past performances, that might be
viewed as sluggish. Nevertheless, his earnings topped $14 mil-
lion, placing him behind only Steve Asmussen at $27 million.
And Asmussen, who started nearly three times the amount of
horses Pletcher did, trained two-time Horse of the Year Curlin,
who won nearly $5.4 million (including his win in the Dubai
World Cup) in 2008.

When asked if he thought some of his rivals are jealous of his
success, Pletcher responded, "I don't think so, I know so. I think
it is just human nature. Plus I grew up in the horse business; I
know [jealousy] is not isolated to one region. It's part of the deal.
I kind of keep to myself anyway, so I'm not out there running
for a popularity contest, or what have you, with the other trainers. I try to be friendly and cordial with everybody. That part
doesn't really bother me, but the part that does bother me is
when people insinuate that you are cheating."

Pletcher finds it especially galling when racing writers take
what he calls "unnecessary shots" at him, because "they don't
come out here and see what is going on. They write from somewhere else."

He recalled an instance in 2004 when a columnist predicted
that he and Bobby Frankel would not do well at that year's
Breeders' Cup due to tighter security measures.

"So after Speightstown won and Ashado won and [Frankel's]

Ghostzapper won the Classic, you never hear anything about the wins," he said. "That type of stuff bothers me; mainly the insinuation that the reason we are not going to do well is because of heightened security and we cheat. That I have a problem with."

Pletcher's three Breeders' Cup winners—Ashado, Speightstown, and English Channel—were ridden by John Velazquez. The trainer-rider combo is one of the most productive in the business. Through 2008, Velazquez had ridden 41 percent of Pletcher's 2,196 career winners.

Velazquez's agent, the retired Hall of Fame rider Angel Cordero Jr., breezes horses for Pletcher, and while the trainer says it helps that Cordero can convey his observations to Velazquez as a result, ultimately it is Pletcher's responsibility to provide jockeys with information that can aid them in a race.

"I think for me as a trainer it is one of the biggest roles you play when you give instructions to riders," he said. "I don't try to handcuff my jockeys too much with, 'I want you here the early part of the race, or I want you laying third, be inside or outside.' I try not to give them too many instructions that way, but I do like to tell them some of the things we might pick up in the mornings that might be helpful to them: if a horse doesn't like dirt in his face or this horse is a little bit difficult with switching over to his right lead. Little things; like maybe the horse isn't that quick away from the gate. I want to tell jockeys those things so they are mentally prepared for them."

While Pletcher usually prefers to use exercise riders when breezing his horses, he feels that it is beneficial to have a jockey aboard a 2-year-old who is being prepared for his career debut.

"We do a little bit of everything, but we probably use exercise riders more than jockeys," Pletcher said. "As a rule, the jockeys want to go a little bit quicker than we want to go. But a 2-year-old getting to run for the first time . . . then it is pretty helpful to have jockeys come out and work them from the gate; maybe get to know them or sharpen them up getting away from the gate."

When possible, Pletcher likes to let his horses have a strong gallop without the pony as they break out of the post parade.

"If we think we have a jockey who is capable of doing it properly, one that I don't have to worry about falling off, and the horse is going to cooperate and not run off, a lot of times I like to take them away from the pony and give them a proper warm-up," he said. "I want to boost them up. I want their heart rate pumping. I want to make sure when they get to the gate they are fully loosened up and ready to roll.

"We have been pretty fortunate that as much as we do it, we have had minimal problems. We've had a couple instances where riders have come off and we've had to scratch. But sometimes that has even happened with the pony. If we have one we worry about being too aggressive and who is going to leave the gate on fire, we might do nothing, and just walk that horse next to the pony, and be as quiet as possible. It depends on the individual horse probably more than anything."

Pletcher loves the business he has chosen, but there is a downside: the arduous task of maintaining a balance between work and family. He is married and has three young children—two sons, Kyle and Payton, and a daughter, Hannah. Pletcher said his wife, Tracy, whom he met in high school and married in 1993, had a notion of what racetrack life was like because her father was in the military.

"I think Tracy knew what she was getting into, but didn't at the same time," Pletcher said with a laugh. "Her father was in the air force, so she had to move around a lot, but it also was a five-day-a-week job, where weekends were leisure time.

TODD PLETCHER

VITAL STATISTICS

CATEGORY	STS.	W%	ROI
1stNAStart	9	0.11	0.73
1stRaceTrn	45	0.13	1.32
180+Trn	88	0.15	1.27
61-180Trn	137	0.2	1.25
2nd45-180Lay	148	0.16	1.22
2nd180+Lay	62	0.16	1.08
1stStart	168	0.15	1.5
2ndMdn	118	0.23	1.7
MSWtoMCL	31	0.1	0.64
1stTurf	95	0.11	1.02
1stBlink	51	0.25	2.63
1stLasix	13	0.08	0.51
2YO	275	0.16	1.18
Dirt/Turf	54	0.13	1.06
Turf/Dirt	81	0.15	1.2
BlinkOn	58	0.26	2.51
BlinkOff	24	0.17	0.62
Sprint/Route	138	0.22	1.69
Route/Sprint	66	0.27	2.17
31-60Days	411	0.23	1.69
WonLast	218	0.18	1.48
Wet	104	0.17	1.17
Dirt	521	0.21	1.66
Turf	453	0.18	1.37
Sprints	393	0.21	1.6
Routes	787	0.18	1.44
MCL	69	0.19	1.22
MSW	399	0.2	1.67
Claim	69	0.28	2.01
ALW	298	0.19	1.36
STK	338	0.16	1.33
GSTK	193	0.15	1.2
DebutMCL	10	0	0
Debut>=1Mile	51	0.12	1.92
Synth	206	0.17	1.34
Turf/Synth	33	0.09	0.61
Synth/Turf	41	0.22	2.53

*January 1, 2008, through February 8, 2009, North American runners only

CAREER HIGHLIGHTS

BREEDERS' CUP

STARTS	1ST	2ND	3RD
55	3	6	8

WINNERS
Ashado: Distaff (2004)
Speightstown: Sprint (2004)
English Channel: Turf (2007)

TRIPLE CROWN

STARTS	1ST	2ND	3RD
32	1	3	4

WINNERS
Rags to Riches: Belmont (2007)

ECLIPSE AWARDS
Leading Trainer (2004-07)
Left Bank: Older Male (2002)
Ashado: 3-Year-Old Filly (2004);
  Older Filly or Mare (2005)
Speightstown: Sprinter (2004)
Fleet Indian: Older Filly or Mare (2006)
Wait a While: 3-Year-Old Filly (2006)
English Channel: Male Turf Horse (2007)
Lawyer Ron: Older Male (2007)
Rags to Riches: 3-Year-Old Filly (2007)

RECORDS/NOTABLE ACHIEVEMENTS
Set North American record for purses won in 2005 ($20,882,842).

Set North American record for purses won in 2006 ($26,882,243).

Set North American record for purses won in 2007 ($28,111,697).

Set North American record for stakes won in 2006 (100).

Set North American record for graded stakes won in 2006 (57).

Reached 2,000 career wins with On the Virg on January 13, 2008, at Santa Anita.

CAREER SUMMARY

STS.	1ST	2ND	3RD	EARNINGS
10,130	2,214	1,641	1,294	$157,660,086

*Through February 8, 2009, North American runners only

"That's the toughest part with the traveling and having a family. One good thing about our business is kids can come to the races. My kids are getting old enough now that they can come to the barn in the summer and weekends. That is helpful. It's not like some guys in similar situations when they are working in Manhattan and travel a lot and their kids can never come to their office. At least on occasion, if they want to, my kids can come out and participate and go to the races. I try to sneak in a few more afternoons off than I used to. Try to attend soccer games, and stuff like that. But it's a challenge."

Eight

Nick Zito

Racing is a cyclic business. Good runs come to sudden halts. Winners evaporate and losers mount. Slumps are part of the game, and trainers are not immune to them. But just as swiftly, a stable can gain momentum. After all, it only takes one good horse to turn things around.

D. Wayne Lukas's powerhouse stable ruled the leader board in New York in 1988 and 1989. At the same time, Nick Zito's barn was experiencing an acute case of seconditis, and as a result, he was getting some good-natured razzing from Lukas's New York assistant, Kiaran McLaughlin. As playful as the comments might have been, they were starting to rankle Zito.

"I was up and down with claiming horses, back and forth," Zito said. "I had a few good outfits. Sandra Payson gave me a break in the late 1980s. I had Ride Sally for her and she won the Top Flight. A couple years earlier, I got this owner

Giles Brophy. Brophy and I went and bought some yearlings and 2-year-olds. But it was hard. I remember being in the receiving barn, and I was literally going to deck Kiaran McLaughlin because he was teasing me to no end. Not really teasing, more like ribbing me. Man, so I walked over to him and said, 'You want your face pushed in?'" And then Zito's luck changed.

At the 1988 Keeneland September yearling sale, Brophy spent $92,000 for a Slew o' Gold colt selected by Zito. A year and a half later, Thirty Six Red won the Wood Memorial and Gotham, then became Zito's first Kentucky Derby starter. Although he finished ninth at Churchill, he would go on to run second to Go and Go in the Belmont Stakes, and finished third to Derby winner and 3-year-old champion Unbridled in the Breeders' Cup Classic.

Thirty Six Red was named for the highest number on the roulette wheel, but Zito doesn't think the colt's name had anything to do with the upswing in his career. He believes it was divine intervention.

The son of a devotedly religious woman, Zito is partial to referencing God after big wins and losses. He said after having a "talk" with God, his fortunes changed.

"One day, I'm walking through Aqueduct's tunnel to the receiving barn," Zito said. "So I'm walking there, and I look up to the sky and the sun is going down. I said, 'Well, God, if you don't want me to make it in a big way, don't worry about it. You have been so good to me, who cares. I understand.' Immediately, here comes Thirty Six Red—immediately. I haven't looked back since. Yes, we have had some ups and downs, but I'm still in business."

Zito, who turned 60 in 2008, saddled his first winner, Palais, in 1972 at the now-defunct Liberty Bell in Pennsylvania. He received his early education on the track while working in the barns of Johnny Campo, Buddy Jacobson, and LeRoy Jolley. A solid claiming trainer for the first 18 years of his career, with a sprinkling of stakes winners, Zito rose to national prominence in 1990 with Thirty Six Red. Since then his name has become synonymous with Triple Crown success: two Kentucky Derby wins, a Preakness, and two Belmonts.

Zito is probably almost as famous for his two victories in the Belmont Stakes as for his dual Derby triumphs, because in both of those Belmonts, he spoiled the Triple Crown bid of a heavy favorite. In 2004, Birdstone shocked the nation when he ran down Smarty Jones. Four years later, Da' Tara stunned Big Brown and the rest of the Belmont field by leading from start to finish. Birdstone, owned by Marylou Whitney, returned $74; Da' Tara, owned by Robert LaPenta, paid $79. In both those Belmonts, Zito also saddled the third-place finishers—Royal Assault in 2004, and Anak Nakal in 2008.

Da' Tara and Anak Nakal elevated Zito's number of Belmont starters to 20, the most of any trainer in the race's history—even more than Lukas, who had saddled 19 runners in the final leg of the Triple Crown through 2008.

While it was great to win two Belmonts on his home track, there is nothing like winning America's most famous horse race, and Zito was over the moon with his two Kentucky Derby triumphs: Strike the Gold in 1991 for the partnership of Brophy, William Condren, and Joseph Cornacchia, and the Condren-and-Cornacchia-owned Go for Gin in 1994. Zito also won the 1996 Preakness with Louis Quatorze for Condren and Cornacchia, and their partner, Georgia Hofmann. Six Zito starters have finished second in the Belmont Stakes.

Strike the Gold, a son of Alydar, was bought by Brophy, Condren, and Cornacchia for $500,000 at auction when he was a yearling. Zito became completely smitten with the handsome chestnut colt, whom he nicknamed Strikey. He often told the media, "He's America's horse."

After winning the Derby, however, Strike the Gold embarked on a 12-race losing streak. The drought led to a dispute among his owners, who began to feud over who would call the shots with the colt. As a result, 12 months after winning the Derby, Strike the Gold went through the ring at a Fasig-Tipton sale at Belmont Park. The auctioneer announced to the large crowd who crammed the sales tent, "Strike the Gold creates auction history by being the first Kentucky Derby winner offered at auction."

The bidding started and Brophy took his shot, but bowed out at $2.45 million. Cornacchia and Condren signed the sales slip for $2.9 million. Four days after the sale, Strike the Gold, with Zito still at the helm, snapped his losing streak by winning the Grade 1 Pimlico Special on May 10, 1992, his first victory since May 4, 1991, in the Derby. He raced until he was 5, and retired to stud with earnings of $3.4 million.

Before Strike the Gold had made his first start, Zito said he saw something special in him. He recalled telling Jenny Kellner, a racing writer, that Strike the Gold was the real deal and a candidate for Kentucky Derby glory.

"You try to find out if the horse has talent in early summer [during their 2-year-old year]," Zito said. "Now, they may not be ready then to run. I showed Jenny Kellner Strike the Gold in this barn at Saratoga when he was a 2-year-old. I said, 'Jenny, this is going to be a good horse.' He was a big, fat 2-year-old. He worked a couple times, not fast, but we still knew he would be good. Jenny said, 'How do you know?' I said, 'I just know.'"

Zito finds it difficult to explain how he developed his sixth sense when assessing a young horse's ability. Perhaps that is because it is tricky to put intuition into words.

"It's a horse's training and demeanor," he said. "Demeanor is a lot. No offense to the people that work for me, but when a horse doesn't work fast, and I know he is a good horse, they can't see it. I can. 'Demeanor' is a great word.

"Take Anak Nakal and Da' Tara, they ran one-two in a maiden race at Belmont in September [2007]. Then they ran one-three in the Belmont Stakes. Isn't that something? You know something about where you are at with a young horse."

Zito is a student of bloodlines, and has no trouble rattling off the pedigrees of horses he trains, those trained by others, and long-dead horses. He said the legendary Greentree Stable's impact on Thirty Six Red's pedigree was the reason he advised Brophy to buy the colt.

"He had the great Greentree blood on the dam side, so it was easy for me," Zito said. "His dam, Heartbreak, was out of Royal Folly. Tom Fool was Royal Folly's sire. It was the real Greentree blood, so that was tremendous.

"I'm a nut for pedigrees. I know the families. In Da' Tara's pedigree, there are two horses in the first and second dams that I know well. The mother of Da' Tara, Torchera, is a daughter of Kaylem Ho, who is the dam of It's So Simple, who won $380,000. He was a hard-knocking horse I trained. I ran him in the Sir Barton, and he ran third. Then he became a top claimer. Then I had another filly, who later was turned over to Sal Russo, Wishful Splendor, who was a stakes horse. A hard-knocker who won $200 grand and was a winner in New York. I trained them both. So I go a long way back with the horses; I know the family whether I trained them or not. I know all the farms. I can tell you every Claiborne mare and Lane's End mare. That's what I do. It's about knowing real horses."

It might seem funny that a kid who grew up in a blue-collar

neighborhood in Queens, not far from Aqueduct, would develop such enthusiasm for Thoroughbred bloodlines. Zito's father, Tom, worked for the city of New York, and for eight years was the chauffeur to Mayor Robert Wagner. Tom introduced Zito, the youngest of his four sons, to the track by bringing him there before he was a teenager. At first, Zito was too young to gain access, and stood with the security guard at the entrance of Aqueduct, waiting for his father, but he quickly figured out how to get into the track.

"When I got a little bit older, I jumped the fence," Zito said. "I used to run in the grandstand at Aqueduct."

His mother, Carmela, a homemaker, died in 2000 at 89, and Zito was hit hard by the loss of the woman who he said "was a great lady; tremendous. What a good person. Very religious; that's where I get some of that from."

Zito's father liked horses so much that he approached Max Hirsch, one of the leading New York trainers in the 1930s and 1940s, for a job, but World War II came and Tom's calling was not at the track, but in the army.

"I am always rooting for the underdog," Zito said. "You know why? My father instilled that in me. So I like whoever the underdog is."

Zito plays the underdog role well. After upsetting Smarty Jones in the 2004 Belmont, Zito apologized to John Servis, the colt's trainer. Zito was aware that the record crowd at Belmont was pulling for Smarty Jones to become racing's first Triple Crown winner since Affirmed in 1978. Smarty Jones nearly gave the 120,139 fans what they came to see. He was on his way to making history when Birdstone came flying late to reel him in. Birdstone's one-length victory spoiled the "Smarty Party," and Zito said he truly felt bad about that.

The circumstances surrounding Da' Tara's Belmont victory

were entirely different, but Zito behaved just as modestly after that win. "I salute Big Brown," he said at the post-race press conference. "He's still a champion, and he wasn't himself today. We took advantage of that." Zito, however, wasn't looking for Big Brown's trainer, Richard Dutrow Jr., to offer apologies, as he had with Servis.

Although Big Brown was a remarkable horse, many people found Dutrow's unabashed confidence off-putting. The trainer repeatedly scoffed at the notion that any horse in the Belmont could beat Big Brown and said a win by his colt was "a foregone conclusion."

Sixteen days after Da' Tara won the Belmont Stakes, Zito reflected upon the outcome of the race, and its aftermath.

"Dutrow opened his mouth," Zito said. "'Big Brown can't lose' . . . this and this. And what happened? So there was no sad. Nobody was really heartbroken over this one because you have to be humble. This is a humbling sport.

"I wasn't apologetic because I didn't think there was any reason to be apologetic. I remember this like yesterday: I went to John Servis and said, 'I'm sorry.' He said, 'What are you talking about? You did a great job.' This is a guy who just wins two-thirds of the Triple Crown, and just gets beat in the Belmont Stakes.

"The other guy is completely the opposite. He says that John Servis did a bad job with Smarty Jones. So it just shows you how this stuff came back and haunted Dutrow. I gave Dutrow a pass, like everyone else, but I didn't give him a pass on one thing: He knocked the horses; that was no good. In other words, that was a no-no. He overstepped the line.

"Let's say I'm your trainer, whether your horse is good, bad, or indifferent, you love that horse. You don't want anyone knocking him or her. Right or wrong? I, as a trainer, have to defend the owner, right or wrong?"

During interviews with Zito, the over-under on how many times he will say "right or wrong" will probably hit the over every time. Zito mixes metaphors, has malapropism down to a science, and mangles quotes from Shakespeare. He also likes to make analogies, which sometimes are difficult to follow, but he can laugh at himself and his comments.

"I say so many things and I don't know what they are. I have to ask you guys to figure them out."

But the trainer always gets his message across, whether he is talking about his horses, the state of the racing industry, or life. He is not short on opinions, and is willing to share his thoughts on just about everything.

Before the Belmont, Dutrow had sparked widespread controversy by blithely announcing that Big Brown, like the rest of the horses in his stable, at one time received a monthly injection of the anabolic steroid Winstrol. After the race, Zito was asked by the media if he used anabolic steroids on Da' Tara and other horses in his barn. Surprisingly, given his usually open nature, Zito declined comment. He said the reason he didn't respond to the question was that he doesn't believe trainers are qualified to address the issue.

"The reason I don't like to answer that question is because it is a medical question," Zito explained. "It's not a trainer question. Over my short life span, when I answer some questions like that, I feel bad in the end, because I don't think I am qualified, and I don't want to sound like a Dutrow when he said, 'Oh, I don't know what [steroids] do.'"

Zito said trainers are put on the hot seat far more often than veterinarians, which he thinks is unfair because the vets are the ones administering the medication, and in some cases, recommending its use. It is illegal for any person at a racetrack to inject a horse, other than a veterinarian.

"If I gave one of these horses a shot, I would kill him because I don't know what I am doing," Zito said. "So who gives them a shot? The vet. Who gives the steroids? The vet. Who gives the other goofy stuff they get? The vet. So a vet needs to be responsible, like a trainer. Shakespeare is right. Remember when he said, 'Look, what do you want for them? It's just merchants, not lawyers or doctors.'"

A Google search for that Shakespeare quote failed to yield any hits, as did a perusal of the venerable resource *Bartlett's Familiar Quotations*. But once you get the hang of it, it's easy to sift through Zito-speak.

"These are just horse trainers. What do you want from them?" he continued. "You need these vets involved. Right or wrong?"

In 36 years of training, Zito has had only one medication positive. The incident occurred in 2000, when a urine test for Mark's Miner came up positive for lidocaine, a local anesthetic, after the horse finished second in a maiden claiming race at Saratoga. Zito still maintains that he was innocent. He was so incensed by the New York State Racing and Wagering Board's ruling that he appealed the case in court. He lost. He also waged an $8 million lawsuit against the board, but eventually dropped the suit when New York's highest court, the court of appeals, refused to hear the case. After a nearly three-year legal battle, he finally took a 10-day suspension.

What particularly upset Zito was that the board came to its decision despite the fact that hearing officer George Dranichak, board chemist Dr. George Maylin, and New York Racing Association steward David Hicks all recommended that Zito be fined, not suspended.

"Now, let me tell you my beef," he said eight years later, still steaming about the whole ordeal. "They told me I had some kind of [topical] cream that got into the horse's system. I went to the hearing officer from the state. Let me tell you how this works, they have a lawyer for the state, the hearing officer from the state, and my lawyer. So it is always two against one. Nobody wins. There was nothing in the blood. It was like a grain of salt; that's how small the level was."

Zito says that he shipped Mark's Miner to Saratoga because the racing secretary needed to fill a race there, and the horse went into a temporary receiving barn.

"He wasn't even in my care," Zito said. "Dr. Maylin testified that the horse licked a bandage. The state racing wagering board, because of the name I had, said, 'No, we've got to do something.' They were using their power."

Though Zito seems like the quintessential New York guy, he loves Kentucky. When he is in Louisville for the Derby, he likes to hang out at the lunch counter at Wagner's, near Churchill Downs, and is practically an honorary citizen of Louisville. He has also had great success at Keeneland, in Lexington—or at least he did before Keeneland installed Polytrack in 2006. Zito won three consecutive fall meets (2003-05) and two spring meets (1997 and 2006). He is an outspoken opponent of synthetic racing surfaces, however, and since the debut of Keeneland's Polytrack in October 2006, he has scaled back dramatically on sending horses there.

Zito, who had won a combined 16 stakes at Keeneland's spring and fall meets through 2007, only ran two horses there during the 2008 spring stand, both in the Blue Grass. Stevil finished fourth and Cool Coal Man was ninth.

The Blue Grass has been a popular Derby prep for Zito, and through 2008, nine of his 21 Derby starters ran in it. Strike the Gold, Halory Hunter, and The Cliff's Edge were all winners.

His other Blue Grass runners who went on to run in the Derby were A P Valentine, Cool Coal Man, Diligence, Louis Quatorze, Suave Prospect, and Sun King.

"I don't like the synthetic tracks," Zito said. "Here is what I think, especially Keeneland, which I love, so it is really hard for me. You know these people were good to me in Kentucky, and I had to be one of the first actually to speak out against synthetics, and I was right. I told them there wasn't enough data, enough information. It's not the answer.

"But here is the problem we got, especially Keeneland. If you look at the Polytrack, most of those horses [winning on it] are better suited to grass. People say, 'That's not true.' Really? If you go look at all the big races being run at Keeneland now on the Polytrack, you will not believe what you see. Most of the horses have grass pedigrees, and nine out of 10 times when they run back on dirt, you can't find them. For instance, just look at the last few years; you get horses like Chatain, trained by Angel Penna Jr. He ran in the Ben Ali. Chatain could have beaten those horses that day, standing still. Thirty lengths he would beat them on conventional dirt." (Chatain finished eighth.)

"Now, let's take the Kentucky Derby," Zito continued. "The last horse to win the Blue Grass and the Kentucky Derby was Strike the Gold. Now, with the synthetics you got the Blue Grass winner, Monba, and the Lane's End winner at Turfway Park, Adriano. One is by A.P. Indy [Adriano] and one is by Maria's Mon [Monba]. They are well-bred horses. Adriano runs 19th in the Kentucky Derby, and Monba runs 20th.

"Now, where am I going with this? Where I am going with this is you're affecting the whole game. The breeding end of it is affected. Wait a minute, how am I [breeding] to Monba, a Grade 1 synthetic horse? Or how am I breeding to Adriano, another possible grass horse with a Grade 2 synthetic win? It's

200 years you are breeding horses on dirt, for what? Speed and endurance. Really when you look at it, this is American racing. So really, unless you're looking at giving it back to the English and French, go ahead, because that is where you are leading to with synthetic tracks.

"I'm going to have to kick and scream to the end. There is research done on synthetics and the breakdowns are the same [as on conventional tracks]. Again, there is not enough information, and then they get hind-end issues on synthetic surfaces. How could I, being somewhat of a spokesman to rescue horses, not want to help horses? Of course I do. But synthetics are not the answer."

Zito and his wife, Kim, are actively involved in horse rescue and in the pursuit of finding homes for Thoroughbreds when they are no longer able to compete and aren't suited for careers in the breeding shed. He demands that vets who work in his barn sign a document that acknowledges they are opposed to horse slaughter.

In 2008, Suffolk Downs instituted a program that bans trainers from the grounds of the Boston track if they are found to have sold horses to a slaughterhouse. Zito was such an admirer of the policy that it was one of the reasons he took Tracy Farmer's two-time Whitney winner Commentator there to race in the Massachusetts Handicap on September 20. After Commentator won, Zito dedicated the victory to a friend who had died two weeks earlier, John Hettinger, a longtime owner and breeder who was a passionate advocate of horse rescue and an opponent of horse slaughter.

Commentator's accomplishments demonstrate that although Zito is best known for his touch with young horses, he also has a knack for keeping old warriors going strong. As a 7-year-old in 2008, Commentator turned in a stirring performance to win the

Whitney by 4¾ lengths for the second time in four runnings—he also won it as a 4-year-old in 2005—and became the second-oldest winner in the race's 81-year history. (Kelso won the Whitney as an 8-year-old in 1965.)

Wanderin Boy, another likeable veteran trained by Zito, won more than $1.2 million for owner Arthur Hancock III but suffered a life-ending injury in the 2008 Cigar Mile at Aqueduct, his 25th career start. He was 7 at the time. Two months later, Zito, who had nursed Wanderin Boy through myriad physical problems during his career, was still shook up over the horse's death.

"It was the last race of his career," he said. "Everyone raved about how great he was doing. That is the really sad thing. The Aqueduct main track is the greatest track in the world. Something went wrong, right? He must have misstepped or something."

Horses like Commentator and Wanderin Boy are throwbacks to an era when racing careers typically lasted longer than they do today. The key to keeping an older horse at his peak, says Zito, is that "anytime you have a shot to make them happy, go ahead and do that. Figure out how to space his training and give him a couple days off when he needs it. Monitor his health, day and night, which we do."

Also, he said it doesn't hurt to have owners who understand that a horse can't make every dance, which helps extend that runner's longevity on the racetrack.

"I have had a lot of horses since they were babies, like Commentator and Wanderin Boy," Zito said. "Hopefully Da' Tara, who I have had since he was a baby, will run until he is 5 or 6. We've had Anak Nakal since he was a baby, and hopefully he will run until he is 5 or 6. You know, we're proud of that because it shows you we take care of them; that's for sure."

He added that "the economical aspect of this game doesn't always give you the opportunity to do that, so you have to have the right people to own the horses. The Farmers, the Hancocks, the Whitneys, Kassem [Masri], those are the right people. You've got to have those people or you are not going to have 7-year-olds racing."

Zito is a proponent of conditioning his horses at Saratoga, before and after the six-week racing meet, and he maintains a division there—primarily his 2-year-olds and stakes horses—during the spring and fall, when the facility remains open for training. Zito himself stays in Saratoga during those months, and usually makes treks on the weekends to check on his Belmont Park division, which is managed by his longtime assistant, Tim Poole.

Although many of New York's top trainers now operate stables at Saratoga during the off-season, Zito was one of the first to take advantage of the peaceful atmosphere upstate, which is particularly apparent when the track is shuttered for racing. In the 1990s, the New York Racing Association opened Saratoga for training in the off-season to accommodate horsemen who had more horses than stalls at Belmont or Aqueduct. The Oklahoma training track is praised for its deep cushion, which is thought to be kinder to horses while also building their stamina. Many of the trainers who use Saratoga as a training center do so with youngsters or lay-up horses. Zito, however, keeps the best of the approximately 80 horses he trains there under his watchful eye.

His barn is one of the most desirable on the Oklahoma backstretch. The roomy stable is close to the training track, but far enough away to be considered quieter than many of the barns that dot the perimeter of the track. Rather than facing the noisy and sometime chaotic scene associated with the training track,

Zito's barn overlooks an open and grassy field, and offers a spectacular view of the sunrise.

"Bill Mott has been here forever, but I would have to say the better horses training here, we started that," Zito said in June 2008. "We have had two Belmont winners pull out of here three days before the race—Birdstone and Da' Tara. Saratoga is like the European way; they train at those yards and they ship in to race. Saratoga is like a tremendous yard that they have in Europe. It used to be one of the best-kept secrets. Here we are now, one month away from the meet, and it used to be there would be hardly anyone here. And look at the stables now that are up here—McGaughey, Mott, Clement, McLaughlin, Pletcher, Contessa, and Weaver. And I'm leaving a bunch out.

"They say you're a product of your environment. Developing horses need that kind of environment. It's our secret, and now everyone seems to realize it is true."

Zito winters his horses in Florida. He prefers Gulfstream to any other track to prepare his 3-year-olds for a possible assault on the Kentucky Derby.

"I haven't gone the Louisiana or California route," Zito said, noting that several of his owners are Floridians. He also feels that Gulfstream "is really the only place to condition 3-year-olds. It's funny, you run in a one-other-than at Gulfstream, and I would say 99 out of 100 times, it becomes a [steppingstone] to a Grade 3 or a Grade 1. That is how tough it is there. If you have a 3-year-old and you develop it in Florida, and they do well, it is a good barometer of their ability."

One of the job requirements of being a trainer is having the ability to handle the ups and downs of the game, and in 2005, Zito had more than his share.

He saddled a record-setting five horses for different owners in the Kentucky Derby, but the best finish among his quintet came from favorite Bellamy Road, who ran seventh. His other starters finished eighth (Andromeda's Hero); 10th (High Fly); 14th (Noble Causeway); and 15th (Sun King) in a 20-horse field. It was an utter Derby downer, but good tidings came on May 31, when it was announced that Zito would be inducted into racing's Hall of Fame.

That same spring, Zito was stunned to find out that 15 horses owned by Marylou Whitney were going to be trained by his former assistant, Reynaldo Abreu. Only a year earlier, Zito had won the Belmont and Travers for Whitney with Birdstone, who also won the Champagne as a 2-year-old. In 2003, Birdstone's half-sister, Bird Town, was victorious in the Kentucky Oaks and the Acorn, and earned the divisional championship.

Zito was shocked that Whitney, racing's most prominent socialite and the widow of the late C. V. Whitney, wanted to break up a winning team, but she and her third husband, John Hendrickson, told Zito they wanted a private trainer for their stable. Zito is still at a loss to explain their decision, but said he remains friends with Whitney and Hendrickson and hopes to train for them again someday. He said he was Whitney's pick for the private-trainer position, but with so many other longtime clients in his stable, such an arrangement would not have been viable.

"After five years working with Marylou, she and John wanted a private trainer," Zito said. "Unfortunately, I don't know what happened. I have no idea where that came from. You have to get Andy Warhol to figure that one out. I really hated to lose them. It's hard to lose a Whitney. She actually wanted me, but I couldn't do it. I wanted to because she is one of my favorites for a lot of reasons, and obviously, for a lot of good reasons. We had some tremendous success together. It would be great to have someone pay all the bills, but in this day and age, no one is getting a private trainer. You just can't. It is not feasible [for a trainer with a big stable]. It's just a hard thing to do."

Zito has trained for a multitude of well-heeled and high-profile owners, including New York Yankees owner George Steinbrenner, who raced 2005 Wood Memorial winner Bellamy Road, and Rick Pitino, the basketball coach for the University of Louisville, who campaigned graded winners Halory Hunter and A P Valentine. Zito has also enjoyed productive associations with Da' Tara's owner, Robert LaPenta; Tracy Farmer, whose stakes winners include Commentator and Albert the Great; Arthur Hancock, who owned Wanderin Boy; and Kassem Masri, owner of Anak Nakal.

LaPenta, a successful businessman whose company, L-1 Identity Solutions, provides advanced solutions for protecting personal identities and assets, entered the game in 1998 when he partnered with Pitino on some horses. He started his own stable in 2001, with Zito at the controls. LaPenta primarily likes to buy yearlings and then try to resell them at a profit, with Zito advising him on which horses to purchase. In 2003, LaPenta bought a Fusaichi Pegasus yearling colt for $270,000 and then sold him the following year at auction for $4.5 million, a record price at the time for a 2-year-old in training. The horse, named Fusaichi Samurai, went on to win only a maiden race, and then became a pleasure horse.

LaPenta has also been lucky with the horses he has kept—those who either didn't bring their reserve price or became injured before a sale. The story of Da' Tara was particularly interesting because he didn't fall into either category, and had it not been for Zito telling LaPenta to keep the yearling he bought for $175,000, the colt would have been sent through a 2-year-old sale. But Zito advised LaPenta that the son of Tiznow needed time to mature and shouldn't be rushed into a 2-year-old auction. The trainer described Da' Tara as being "an absolutely spectacular-looking horse" as a youngster.

Another stroke of fortune was that LaPenta was forced to keep War Pass, a $180,000 yearling acquisition, who was bound for a 2-year-old sale but had to be withdrawn when he required surgery to remove ankle chips.

War Pass, a son of Cherokee Run, won the 2007 Champagne and Breeders' Cup Juvenile, and the Eclipse Award. He ended his 2-year-old campaign undefeated in four starts. Will Farish, the owner of Lane's End Farm, bought War Pass's breeding rights after the Breeders' Cup and became LaPenta's partner in the colt for the duration of his racing career.

Zito was feeling that Kentucky Derby mojo with War Pass, but the plan was derailed in April 2008 after War Pass developed a small fracture in his right front sesamoid. He never made it back to the races, and in September 2008 it was announced that he would enter stud the following year at Lane's End in Kentucky.

Before the injury, War Pass easily won an allowance race at Gulfstream, turned in a too-bad-to-be-true performance in the Tampa Bay Derby, finishing last, and then rebounded with a good second to Tale of Ekati in the Wood Memorial.

Zito believes that War Pass injured himself in the Wood because Aqueduct's main track was too deep. The day before the Wood, racing at the Big A was canceled because of heavy rain. It was a huge disappointment for Zito, who said that War Pass, along with Bellamy Road and Unbridled's Song, whom he trained toward the end of the colt's career, possessed more raw talent than any of the other horses he has ever handled.

"Before War Pass won the Champagne, we went like two years without winning any stakes," Zito said. "However, we ran second or third in 18 Grade 1's. If you are down to your last $10,

NICK ZITO

VITAL STATISTICS

CATEGORY	STS.	W%	ROI
1stRaceTrn	4	0	0
180+Trn	17	0.29	2.06
61-180Trn	79	0.2	1.31
2nd45-180Lay	77	0.21	2.06
2nd180+Lay	7	0.29	2.4
1-7Last	1	0	0
1stStart	45	0.07	0.54
2ndMdn	42	0.12	0.77
MSWtoMCL	13	0.15	1.29
1stTurf	12	0	0
1stBlink	24	0.17	1.17
2YO	60	0.12	0.59
Dirt/Turf	13	0	0
Turf/Dirt	8	0.12	0.49
BlinkOn	27	0.19	1.18
BlinkOff	26	0.08	0.63
Sprint/Route	68	0.12	0.94
Route/Sprint	39	0.23	1.18
31-60Days	142	0.16	1.31
WonLast	72	0.32	2.47
Wet	64	0.12	1.31
Dirt	403	0.19	1.57
Turf	13	0	0
Sprints	175	0.2	1.24
Routes	243	0.17	1.71
MCL	47	0.23	1.71
MSW	139	0.13	0.92
Claim	31	0.16	1.01
ALW	111	0.26	1.6
STK	89	0.15	2.37
GSTK	59	0.08	2.43
DebutMCL	5	0	0
Debut>=1Mile	4	0	0
Synth	2	0	0

*January 1, 2008, through February 8, 2009, North American runners only

CAREER HIGHLIGHTS

BREEDERS' CUP

STARTS	1ST	2ND	3RD
22	2	4	3

WINNERS
Storm Song: Juvenile Fillies (1996)
War Pass: Juvenile (2007)

TRIPLE CROWN

STARTS	1ST	2ND	3RD
60	5	8	7

WINNERS
Strike the Gold: Kentucky Derby (1991)
Go for Gin: Kentucky Derby (1994)
Louis Quatorze: Preakness (1996)
Birdstone: Belmont (2004)
Da' Tara: Belmont (2008)

ECLIPSE AWARDS
Storm Song: 2-Year-Old Filly (1996)
Bird Town: 3-Year-Old Filly (2003)
War Pass: 2-Year-Old Colt (2007)

RECORDS/NOTABLE ACHIEVEMENTS
Inducted into racing Hall of Fame (2005).

Snapped D. Wayne Lukas's streak of six consecutive Triple Crown victories by saddling Louis Quatorze to win 1996 Preakness.

Leading trainer at Keeneland four times: spring 1997, fall 2003, 2004 (tie), and 2005.

Won three consecutive runnings of the Grade 1 Champagne Stakes at Belmont Park, with The Groom Is Red (1998), Greenwood Lake (1999), and A P Valentine (2000).

Foiled Triple Crown bids by Smarty Jones (2004) with Birdstone and by Big Brown (2008) with Da' Tara.

Trained Birdstone to win the two biggest races for 3-year-olds in New York in 2004, the Belmont Stakes and the Travers.

Saddled five horses for five different owners in the 2005 Kentucky Derby.

CAREER SUMMARY

STS.	1ST	2ND	3RD	EARNINGS
12,661	1,663	1,569	1,485	$89,401,474

*Through February 8, 2009, North American runners only

chances are you're walking out of the track broke. We were down to the last $10 and somehow War Pass jump-started us again.

"I think this is the most unforgiving business I have seen. It was one of my biggest disappointments what happened with War Pass. Everything has to go right. The great jockey agent Lenny Goodman told me once, 'Don't you forget it, Nick, when you come in the barn in the morning, what you are going to see is not everything nice. There are some mornings where some-one is going to tell you, this horse has this, this one has that.' And you know what? He was right."

Despite his tremendous accomplishments with 3-year-olds, Zito said the disappointments significantly outweigh the success stories. But each new crop of 2-year-olds sends a fresh wave of optimism through the Zito barn.

"I think in my head, I put every horse as a top 3-year-old," he said. "I never lose sight that he could be a good 3-year-old."